INNOCENCE AND DESIGN

The 1985 BBC Reith Lectures

INNOCENCE AND DESIGN

The Influence of Economic Ideas on Policy

David Henderson

Basil Blackwell

© P. D. Henderson 1986

First published 1986

Basil Blackwell Ltd
108 Cowley Road, Oxford OX4 1JF, UK

Basil Blackwell Inc.
432 Park Avenue South, Suite 1505,
New York, NY 10016, USA

British Library Cataloguing in Publication Data

Henderson, David, *1927–*
    Innocence and design: the influence of
    economic ideas on policy. —
    (BBC Reith lectures; 1985)
    1. Economic policy
    I. Title   II. Series
    330.9   HD87

ISBN 0–631–14795–0
ISBN 0–631–14796–9 Pbk

Typeset by Oxford Publishing Services, Oxford
Printed in Great Britain by TJ Press Ltd, Padstow

CONTENTS

Preface   vii

1   The Power of Do-It-Yourself Economics   1

2   Soap Opera in High Places   17

3   Needs, Centralism and Autarchy   36

4   Orthodox Economists versus the People   53

5   DIYE plus the Lobbies: Counting the Cost   73

6   Markets, States and Economics   93

Suggestions for Reading   110

'Sir, I shall be amenable to reason,' said Captain Dalgetty,
'supposing it addresses itself to my honour and my interest.'
(Sir Walter Scott, A Legend of Montrose*)*

PREFACE

This book is an enlarged version of the 1985 BBC Reith
Lectures. In editing the lectures for publication in book
form, I have included a number of passages which were in
one or another of my original drafts, but were omitted or
drastically shortened in order to keep the final broadcast
text within its strictly assigned limits. I have also added
references and some suggestions for reading. The main
argument of the lectures is unchanged.

It is a pleasure to acknowledge the help and guidance
which I have received from many sources in preparing both
the lectures and this book. My first debt is to the
Secretary-General of the OECD, who gave permission for
me to accept the invitation from the Governors of the BBC
to give the 1985 Reith Lectures.

I decided from the outset to illustrate the argument
wherever possible with actual cases and examples. In
choosing and working up these, I drew extensively in some
cases on the expertise of others, who were able to direct me
to published sources or who themselves gave helpful and
informative answers to my questions. Among the many
persons and agencies who contributed in this way, I am
indebted particularly to the various British government
departments to which I wrote asking for assistance, and
which went out of their way to respond.

A number of people read parts of the text in draft, and
made comments and suggestions which greatly improved

the final product. For this my thanks go to Ron Gass, Val Koromzay, David Sawers, Maurice Scott, Jeffrey Shafer and Philip Watts, and to my son John and my wife Marcella.

A special word of acknowledgement is due to my producer, David Morton. Not only did he handle all administrative and editorial aspects impeccably, but his ideas and suggestions were extremely helpful at every stage from the first drafts of the lectures to the final scripts and recordings. A whole host of improvements originated with him. I would also like to thank George Fischer, Head of Talks and Documentaries Radio at the BBC, for his advice and encouragement.

My disordered initial drafts were turned into flawless documents by Jennifer McIntosh, and in her absence by Moya Renshaw.

My title was originally used by Robert Byron and Christopher Sykes for a novel which they published together in 1935. I came across the reference many years ago, when reading the essay on Robert Byron in Christopher Sykes's enjoyable book, *Four Studies in Loyalty*.

The choice and treatment of the subject matter for these Reith Lectures, and the views expressed in them, are mine alone. What is said here does not represent the official position of the OECD, nor for that matter of any of the other organizations in which I have worked.

P. D. Henderson
Paris, November 1985

1

THE POWER OF DO-IT-YOURSELF ECONOMICS

'It is very rarely, if ever, that the practical economic questions which are presented to the statesman can be unhesitatingly decided by abstract reasoning from elementary principles. For the right solution of them full and exact knowledge of the facts of a particular case is commonly required; and the difficulty of ascertaining these facts is such as to prevent the attainment of positive conclusions by any strictly scientific procedure.

At the same time, the function of economic theory in relation to such problems is none the less important and indispensable; since the practical conclusions of the most untheoretical expert are always reached implicitly or explicitly by some kind of reasoning from some economic principles: and if the principles or reasoning be unsound the conclusions can only be right by accident.' (Henry Sidgwick, Principles of Political Economy, *3rd edition, 1901, pp. 7–8)*

John Maynard Keynes's great work, *The General Theory of Employment, Interest and Money*, which was published almost exactly 50 years ago, ends with a justly famous tribute to the influence of ideas on events. The last lines of the book read as follows:

> . . . the ideas of economists and political philosophers, both when they are right and when they are wrong, are more powerful than is commonly understood. Indeed the world is ruled by little else. Practical men, who believe themselves to be quite exempt from any intellectual influences, are

usually the slaves of some defunct economist. Madmen in authority, who hear voices in the air, are distilling their frenzy from some academic scribbler of a few years back. I am sure that the power of vested interests is vastly exaggerated compared with the gradual encroachment of ideas. Not, indeed, immediately, but after a certain interval; for in the field of economic and political philosophy there are not many who are influenced by new theories after they are twenty-five or thirty years of age, so that the ideas which civil servants and politicians and even agitators apply to current events are not likely to be the newest. But, soon or late it is ideas, not vested interests, which are dangerous for good or evil.[1]

I can still remember the excitement, and the sense of conviction, which I felt on first reading these words as a student in Oxford just over 40 years ago. They cast for me a new light on the world, and on the subject that I had begun to try to master.

Not surprisingly, this passage has been quoted many times, and its thesis much debated, by economists and economic historians down the years. How far was Keynes right in those eloquent concluding sentences?

The phenomenon of do-it-yourself economics

My own views on this have been shaped, not just by reading the works of scholars, but also – and in fact largely – by personal experience and observation. The experience has been of working as a professional economist in a number of different roles and countries. I cannot claim to have greatly influenced the course of events; and so far as I know, no practical man has ever shown signs of becoming my intellectual slave. But from my long years either in or close to official bureaucracies, both national and international, I have formed the view that Keynes's famous thesis needs to be amended in at least one respect.

He was right, I think, in the broad direction of his argument. There is no doubt that the policies of governments have been, and still are, strongly influenced by economic ideas. But contrary to what Keynes assumed, these have not necessarily been the ideas of economists. Over wide areas of policy the judgements of politicians and their officials, as also of public opinion in general, have been and still are guided to a large extent by beliefs and perceptions about the working of the economic system, and about national interests and the welfare of the community, which owe little or nothing to the economics profession. In so far as the world is indeed ruled by economic ideas, these are often the intuitive ideas of lay people, rather than the more elaborate systems of thought which occupy the minds of trained economists. The history of national economic policies down the years bears witness not only to the influence of economists, whether defunct or alive, but also to the power of what I call '*do-it-yourself economics*'.

I first became aware of this phenomenon – which I may say came as a complete surprise to me – in the late 1950s, when I spent a year on leave from the academic post which I then held in Oxford, and went to work as an Economic Adviser in Her Majesty's Treasury. This was my first glimpse of economic policy-making from the inside. The experience changed both my view of the world and the direction of my professional interests. I want now to describe what happened, not because I intend to use these lectures as an occasion for autobiography, but because it serves to introduce and illustrate my main theme.

Macroeconomics and the Keynesian ascendancy

I joined the Treasury at the beginning of September 1957. Up to that time, I had seen no reason to doubt the essential truth of what Keynes had said about the relation between economists' ideas and government policies. After all, the very success of his own ideas was evidence that he was right. In Britain, and increasingly in other countries too, the Keynesian revolution had taken hold. Its doctrines had established themselves with remarkable speed, not only within universities but apparently also as the basis for official policy. Like almost every one in my generation of economists in Britain, I approved of this and took heart from it. I assumed, as most of us did, that the chief role of those economists who were interested in questions of policy, and who wished to influence policy whether as officials within the government machine or as commentators outside it, was to ensure that Keynesian ideas were further developed and effectively put into practice.

For some time, what I saw and learned from my new vantage point in Whitehall served only to confirm these beliefs. In the Treasury, I became one of a small group of economists who made up what was then known as the Economic Section. All of us were Keynesians, and very much aware of being so. Moreover, the subjects that we were concerned with, both in official memoranda and in our discussions with one another, the terms of reference of the committees we served on, and indeed the very existence of the Economic Section as such, all to my mind bore witness to Keynes's vision of a world shaped by 'the gradual encroachment of ideas'. They were manifestations of the Keynesian ascendancy.

This ascendancy was both intellectual and practical, and the links between the two were close. As to the intellectual side, the Keynesian revolution had led to the establishment of macroeconomics as a leading, distinctive and unified branch of economic theory, which it still remains. 'Macro' as distinct from 'micro' economics is concerned with the properties and functioning of the economic system as a whole. In particular, it tries to describe, explain and predict changes over time in output or production, employment and unemployment, and the general price level. Its interest is largely in the recent past, and the not too distant future.

If you wanted a professional answer to the questions, 'what's been happening to the economy, and where is it going now?', it is to a macroeconomist that you would turn. These were precisely the main questions that were put to us in the Economic Section, though we often dealt with them as members of substantial teams of officials drawn not only from various parts of the Treasury but also from other departments and from the Bank of England. It was largely on macroeconomic issues that we were employed in the public service.

Applied macroeconomic work, then as now, covers a wide range of issues and topics. These include public sector revenues and expenditures; the main elements of private demand, i.e. consumers' expenditure and business investment; exports and imports; international financial flows, the balance of payments, and the exchange rate; the money supply, interest rates and financial markets; key wage and salary negotiations; and last though not least, the likely course and impact of developments in the world economy generally. But in all this the focus of attention is on the national economy as a whole – or in some cases, such as my own department within the OECD, a group of national economies and their interactions within an international system. Macroeconomics now is less identified with Keynes's work than it was in my far-off Treasury days, and there are deeper professional disagreements within it; but its broad subject matter and concerns remain much the same.

As to the practical connection between Keynesian macroeconomic theory and government policies, this was officially established in Britain in the spring of 1944, when the then wartime coalition government issued a White Paper under the title *Employment Policy*. The opening sentence, which today perhaps has rather a sad ring about it, read as follows: 'The Government accept as one of their primary aims and responsibilities the maintenance of a high and stable level of employment after the war.'[2] This aim was to be achieved by Keynesian means, through financial policies designed to operate on and control the level of *demand* within the economy – that is, the flow of public and private expenditure. Hence the chief single task of economic policy was now conceived as being the management of demand. In the post-war years, this conception of policy and of the role of government was adopted without much internal debate by both the main political parties, with no major differences between them. By the early 1950s the so-called 'Keynesian consensus' had been established, and it was to remain in place until well into the 1970s.

One result of this wider economic role of government was to strengthen the power of the Treasury, which was already the senior Whitehall department. To its traditional functions the Treasury had now added the primary responsibility for policies affecting the economy as a whole, and in particular for the management of demand.

A second result was the establishment in a central position within the British official machine of a small group of economists identified as such. Before 1939 no such group had existed. During the war a number of economists were brought into Whitehall: Keynes himself was one of them. Some worked as professionals, mainly in the Economic Section of the Cabinet Office which was created in 1941. Others were assigned to more general administrative tasks. At the end of the war most of them left the civil service, either to return to universities or to pursue other careers. (Among those in the latter group were Hugh Gaitskell and Harold Wilson, who both entered the House of Commons in 1945.) Of those who stayed, some signed on as regular civil servants in the Administrative Class. A small handful, still identified as professionals, remained in the Economic Section. For a while, their future was uncertain; but as time went on, and financial and more especially budgetary policies became increasingly the main single instrument of the government's economic policy, they found an accepted role. In 1953 the Economic Section was transferred from the Cabinet Office to the Treasury. This change, which formalized working relationships which by then were well established, placed it at the centre of the web of economic policy-making.

Macroeconomics is not the whole of economics, and there are questions of economic policy on which it has little to contribute. But these aspects of theory and policy receded into the background as a result of the Great Depression of the 1930s and the Keynesian revolution. My own view of the world, at the time when I was still a newcomer in Whitehall, was I think widely shared in the profession and by informed people outside it. I thought that issues of macroeconomic policy were of dominant importance; that dramatic advances had been made in the economic theory which bore on these issues; and that thanks to the spread of Keynesian ideas within official circles, together with increasing reliance on professional economic advice, they were now handled with greater knowledge and competence than before, both in Britain and in other developed industrial countries. If asked then what I thought it important still to achieve, I would have replied that the battle of ideas in Washington was not yet won. Keynesian ways of thinking had become generally dominant in American universities, but not as yet at the highest levels within the government. When John Kennedy defeated Richard Nixon in the 1960 presidential election, I was pleased at the result partly because I believed – correctly as it proved – that he was more favourable to the Keynesian approach, and would make his senior economic appointments accordingly.

At this stage, then, I was well aware that there were other questions in economics, that there existed (so to speak) a second tier of economic issues; but my interests were very largely directed towards the first tier, the world of macroeconomics. From observation of this world, I saw every reason to believe that Keynes was right in that often quoted closing paragraph of the *General Theory*. It was indeed the ideas of economists, rather than vested interests, which largely decided the choices that governments made.

Discovering DIYE

However, in the life of a temporary and junior civil servant fate was about to deal a new hand. I mentioned earlier that in assuming the main responsibility for economic management in Britain, the Treasury had enlarged its sphere. Its traditional functions still remained, and these included the control and oversight of public expenditure. Here the Treasury divisions concerned carried on an unceasing argument with the various spending departments. Since our responsibilities, and our professional interests too, were largely on the macroeconomic side, the Economic Section was not much involved in this. But every now and then, when a regular Treasury administrator felt that he needed some help, one of us would be asked to give an opinion or attend a meeting. I was drawn into some of this work by accident; and I found it so interesting that, with the agreement of my superiors, I decided to make it my main activity. In particular, I attended the numerous – and often contentious – meetings of two high-level interdepartmental committees that were appointed at this time to report to ministers on the future of major public expenditure programmes. One was concerned with forestry, and the other with government support for the aircraft industry.

I now found myself in a different world, both administratively and intellectually. For one thing, vested interests were involved in an obvious and indeed essential way. The very make-up of the official committees, and the lines on which the argument was conducted, were evidence of this. Those sitting around the table were there as the accredited representatives of the departments and agencies that were interested parties. Their role was to articulate and defend either the interests of their own organizations, or those of outside groups for which departments acted as sponsors or advocates within Whitehall. Officials appeared not as individuals, but as it were wearing masks, like actors in a Greek drama. Moreover, for some of the interested parties the stakes could be high: the Forestry Commission, for instance, felt at the time – I think with justice – that its very survival might be in question.

Another difference was that the second tier of economics was involved. Here I was dealing with choices relating to particular expenditure programmes, and this meant that I had to think about the general criteria, the yardsticks, which ought to be applied in such choices. I had to go back to the microeconomic theory I had learned as a student and teacher, and see how it might best be brought to bear. As I did so, I was struck by the fact that in this second tier of economic policy discussion, even more than in macroeconomics, the aspects of the questions that an economist could handle just from his own professional training were insufficient to provide the basis for informed judgement. Much more than general economic reasoning was needed. Specialized facts and figures, past history and current technology, a feel for roles and institutions, all these were and are a necessary part of understanding. At the same time, standard economic analysis *was* helpful, more so than I had expected. Last – and this especially came as a surprise – the use of conventional economic ideas often set me apart from other committee members, who revealed themselves as having quite different ways of viewing economic aspects of the issues under consideration. This was true not only of the other departments, but sometimes of Treasury officials too.

Thinking of Keynes's words, I asked myself where these committee table ideas had originated. They did not come from past university economics courses, which in any case few of the officials concerned had attended. Nor were they derived from the present-day writings of economists outside the official machine, if only because Whitehall was – as it remains – very much a self-contained world, generating its own information and ideas. (The brilliant *Yes, Minister* series accurately conveys the feeling of a private universe of ministers and officials, where almost any outsider appears as either a nuisance or a threat.) Finally, there were very few cases in which these ideas could have been picked up from economists within the departments concerned, since – as I now began to observe – units corresponding to the Economic Section were rare outside the Treasury. It was apparent that economists, whether past or present, inside or outside, were simply not involved. The doctrines that I was now encountering were intuitive and self-generated: those who held them thought that what they were saying was plain common sense, which needed no prompting or authority.

I kept thinking about this discovery, both at the Treasury and after my return to Oxford; and in the summer of 1960 I wrote a paper on the subject.[3] I called it 'The Use of Economists in British Administration', but it was really about their non-use. In it I cited for illustrative purposes four cases or areas in which British official policy seemed to have been affected by rather crude economic reasoning; and I referred to them as examples of 'economic policy without economics'. I would now use a different phrase. Economic considerations, as indeed I pointed out in the article, had been present, even dominant, in all four. But the economics which had been brought to bear was not that of the professionals. What I had identified, and perceived as being widespread and influential in Whitehall, was do-it-yourself economics (DIYE for short).

A universal empire of ideas

Although it was in Her Majesty's Treasury that I first came to appreciate the strong persuasive influence that do-it-yourself economics can exert on politicians and their advisers, and indeed on public opinion in general, I soon realized that the Whitehall of the late 1950s was far from being an unusual case. In fact, the leading ideas of DIYE have a universal character: they can be seen across national frontiers and down the centuries. They are unchanging, timeless, and often deeply held. They are the economics of Everyman.

Now from a historical point of view, the notion that economic policies can be chosen and implemented without benefit of economists is not in the least surprising. After all, there are issues of economic policy as old as human society, while economics as a systematic body of thought dates only from the late eighteenth century. For better or for worse, the various experts who advised rulers and governments in earlier times could not have possessed the kind of expertise which an economic training is designed to give. Their ways of thinking, and their perceptions of issues and events, were in this sense *pre-economic*.

What is striking, however, is the prevalence today of very similar modes of thought – for the do-it-yourself economics of 1985, like that of earlier periods, is essentially pre-economic. More than two centuries have passed since the publication of Adam Smith's great treatise, *The Wealth of Nations*; and trained economists are now well established, not just in universities and research institutes, but also in business enterprises, civil services, and the councils of presidents and prime ministers. In Whitehall, for example, the situation has been transformed since the days of my bureaucratic apprenticeship. Yet DIYE has not become a curiosity of the past. All over the world, ideas and beliefs which owe nothing to recognized economics textbooks still retain their power to influence people and events.

This makes economics an unusual case. In most subjects which have become established academic disciplines, the professionals have long since driven the amateurs from the field. Uninstructed 'pre-scientific' notions, where they still survive, are a fringe phenomenon without influence on serious opinion. But with economics, even now, the situation often resembles a case which I came across some five years ago in an article in the *Wall Street Journal*.[4]

The article concerned an American economist, William Niskanen, whom I had the pleasure of meeting last year in Washington, by which time he had become a member of the President's Council of Economic Advisers. Then, however, he had just been dismissed from his post as director of economics at the Ford Motor Co. because he refused to accept or support the company's plea for protection against imports of cars from Japan. Commenting on the incident to the *Wall Street Journal*, Niskanen described one aspect of his experience at Ford in words which I found illuminating, though not at all surprising. He said that:

> In contrast with their attitudes towards lawyers and engineers, (whose expertise is readily accepted), business managers are quick ... to override the judgement of economists on economic matters. Basically, every senior manager and board member of Ford thinks of himself as an economist, as having a democratic right to make his own judgement about economic phenomena.

This account of executive life in Detroit, with every man his own economist, describes a common situation. However, I would add three riders.

First, such a state of affairs is not peculiar to business, but is to be found in government and other walks of life. Second, my distinction between the two tiers of economic discourse has to be borne in mind. Economists are more often asked for their views, and more readily listened to when they express them, on some topics than on others. Third, in my experience it is not so much that the views of economists are brusquely overridden by laymen, though this can happen. More often, it simply does not occur to those who subscribe to intuitive economic ideas that there might actually be an alternative way of thinking, and that the issues they are passing judgement on could be viewed in a different light. In dealing with economic questions, their typical state of mind is one of *innocence*.

I want now to consider the rather surprising persistence of pre-economic ways of thought, and to suggest answers to the following groups of questions.

First, what are the characteristic features and doctrines of do-it-yourself economics? How do they contrast with economists' ways of analysing and assessing the same issues? What are the implications for actual economic policies of adopting one framework of thinking rather than the other?

Next, why is it that in some areas of policy the ideas of economists have little persuasive power, while in others it seems that – to quote again the striking phrase that Keynes used half a century ago – 'the world is ruled by little else'? Is this striking divergence due to some branches of economics having made greater progress than others? Alternatively, can it be explained by differences in the extent to which vested interests, as distinct from ideas, influence what governments decide? Why have the professionals been so unsuccessful in weakening the hold of do-it-yourself economics, where its view of the world and theirs are in conflict?

Finally, how much does it matter if DIYE continues to hold sway? Would the world be a noticeably better place if more distinctively professional views, of the kind I shall describe, carried greater weight than they do at present?

Presenting the two systems

My first task, then, is to sketch out the main ideas of do-it-yourself economics, and show how and why they differ from the ideas of people like me. It is not easy to present either of these two systems adequately and without distortion in what can only be the barest outline. Each of them presents its own problem. In the case of do-it-yourself economics there are naturally no manuals or textbooks to go by, so I have used my own descriptive labels and categories which are necessarily subjective. On the other side of the fence, the main problem – notoriously – is that economists do not speak with one voice: on many of the issues that I shall refer to, the professionals are less united than the amateurs. Some of them are simply not concerned with the kinds of question on which intuition and the standard university textbook are apt to diverge: their expertise, and their professional interests, lie elsewhere in the subject. Others would, on some issues at any rate, actually want to take the side of the amateurs. I have described the characteristic state of mind of do-it-yourself economics as one of innocence, and I think this is just; but a significant number of my professional colleagues, in response to the arguments I am about to present, might be disposed to remind me that in the Hans Andersen story it was precisely the innocence of the child which enabled him to see, and to say out loud, that the emperor had no clothes.

Let me emphasize, therefore, that the economists' approach which I shall outline represents only one tendency, albeit an influential one, within a fragmented and divided profession. I shall call it the *orthodox* or *establishment* view. Its roots lie deep in the history of economic thought, and a systematic economic training usually, though not always, leads people either to accept it or at least to acknowledge its place within the subject. But though distinctively professional, it is viewed by some of the professionals themselves with indifference, lack of enthusiasm or even active hostility. I shall return to these differences of opinion at a later stage.

Partly because of them, I do not put forward the orthodox view as the last word in wisdom. Perhaps I can best indicate the spirit in which I present it now by referring to a comic novel, Thomas Love Peacock's *Crotchet*

Castle, which was published in 1831. In it there appears an allegedly representative economist. Given the period, he is naturally a Scotsman from Edinburgh, the city of David Hume and Adam Smith. His name is Mr MacQuedy – Mac Q.E.D., the son of a demonstration – and he represents the essence, the spirit, of political economy (as economics was then called). In the same way as Peacock, though with more serious intent, I want to convey the essence of a particular approach, a characteristic way of viewing and assessing issues and events. Accordingly, I imagine Mr MacQuedy restored to the scene, in modern dress, with modern orthodox ideas, trying as ever to persuade us to see the world through his eyes. Think of him, if you will, as the exponent and representative of the orthodox economic doctrine of today, and of me in turn as his interpreter.

In thus conjuring up the ghost of Mr MacQuedy, I do not intend to conceal or retreat from my own point of view. He and I largely agree: we are members of the same club. Over the years, my working experience has led me to draw closer to the establishment position; and in comparing it now with do-it-yourself economics, I do not pretend to be impartial. But I want to distance myself a little from him, leaving open the possibility that our views might not always coincide.

Let me add a further disclaimer. In these lectures I shall be concerned with the uses of economics, and by implication therefore with the role of economists; and part of the time I shall speak as an advocate. But I make no extravagant claims on behalf of my subject. Like other experts, economists are sometimes inclined to be condescending in their treatment of laymen, but I believe that as a profession we have little to be condescending about. In that paper of mine which I mentioned, published some 25 years ago, I argued in favour of greater economic expertise in Whitehall, and I think I was right to do so. But I also made two qualifying remarks, which I would like to quote now since they also apply to what I have to say in these lectures. I said, first, that 'no argument put forward here depends on a utopian or even optimistic assessment of the achievements or the potentialities of economics in its application to questions of policy': and in a later footnote to the article I wrote, even more prudently perhaps, that 'the argument . . . does not depend on a favourable assessment of the predictive value of economic models'.[5]

The professional differences which are so apparent within economics have a number of causes, but possibly the main single factor is that the behaviour of economic systems is not well understood. In part, this is because these systems are subject to a process of unceasing change which is unique in time: in the enormously complex economic drama which is continuously being enacted, there are indeed some elements of regularity, but there are no repeat performances. Hence even if economists were more agreed on what was likely to happen and why, this would not rule out the possibility that future developments would challenge or discredit these accepted views.

For this and other reasons, economic policy – to adapt a well known saying – is too serious a matter to be left to economists. But equally, it seems to me, economic policy is too serious a matter to be conducted without reference to the ideas of economists; and this is the theme which Mr MacQuedy will be helping me develop in my next three lectures.

Notes

1 J.M. Keynes, *The General Theory of Employment, Interest and Money*, London, Macmillan, 1936, pp. 383–4.
2 *Employment Policy*, Cmd.6527, London, HMSO, 1944.
3 P.D. Henderson, 'The Use of Economists in British Administration', *Oxford Economic Papers*, vol. 13, no. 1, February 1961.
4 'Ford Fires an Economist', *Wall Street Journal*, 30 July 1980.
5 Henderson, 'The Use of Economists', pp. 13 and 17.

2

SOAP OPERA IN HIGH PLACES

Mr MacQuedy: *Then, sir, I presume you set no value on the right principles of rent, profit, wages, and currency?*
The Rev. Dr Folliott: *My principles, sir, in these things are, to take as much as I can get, and to pay no more than I can help. These are every man's principles, whether they be the right principles or no. There, sir, is political economy in a nutshell.*
Mr MacQuedy: *The principles, sir, which regulate production and consumption, are independent of the will of any individual as to giving or taking, and do not lie in a nutshell by any means. (Thomas Love Peacock,* Crotchet Castle*)*

I have described how my own experience, while working many years ago as a British civil servant, led me to make a distinction between economic ideas in general and the ideas of economists in particular. The first category embraces the second, but it extends more widely. It includes beliefs and perceptions which are unrelated to the characteristic ways of thought of trained economists. These are not supported by any reference to published work, or to the results – such as these may be – of professional economic inquiry. They have a life of their own. Because of this autonomy, and the informality and lack of system which go with it, I have termed this collection of beliefs and perceptions 'do-it-yourself economics'.

In this and the two following lectures, I shall sketch out

the leading elements of DIYE. I shall show how they differ
from ideas that are widely accepted by trained economists,
and consider the implications of these differences for
economic policy. I am not trying to suggest that the
economists' ideas as I present them, which can broadly be
described as orthodox, are shared by every one in our
profession. For the time being professional opinion is
represented only by my fictional colleague Mr MacQuedy,
who is a strict champion of orthodoxy and with whom, on
these issues at any rate, I am happy to associate myself.

In outlining these two approaches, the amateur and the
professional, I shall be drawing on concrete real-life
examples, culled from my well-stocked personal collection.
They will serve to emphasize the point that DIYE has been,
and continues to be, influential with people who are
themselves influential.

Soap operatics in three guises

What are the characteristic ideas and beliefs of do-it-
yourself economics? I treat them here under several rather
disrespectful headings of my own choice, the first of which
is *soap opera*. I mean by this the disposition to ascribe to
particular elements within an economic system – industries, sectors, products, processes or activities – intrinsic
qualities which (it is thought) should influence the way in
which governments treat them. I use the term because I
believe that this approach to economic issues resembles the
script of a soap opera both in its crude assumptions and in
its failure to reflect the complexities of real life. Soap
operatics takes three main forms. First, there is the
conception of *manifest economic destiny*. This merges into the
second, which I shall label – borrowing the term from Peter
Wiles's excellent book, *Communist International Economics*[1] –
structure snobbery. The third I call *essentialism*. Let me present

a few instances of each, together with some of the official policies that are based on them.

Ideas of manifest economic destiny provide the script for grand soap operatics, in which features or component parts of an economic system are cast in historic roles. Thus in an article on issues confronting the European Community which he contributed to *The Times* two years ago, the then Prime Minister of France, M. Pierre Mauroy, laid down the following as the first of 'some fundamental points [on which] we cannot compromise':

> European agriculture must in future be able to realize its full potential and to confirm its vocation as an exporter in order to play its part in the balance of our current account, and to fulfil its duty to the Third World.[2]

In this case, as often happens, the operatics were closely linked with another leading element of DIYE, namely *traditional mercantilism* – that is, the notion that an increase in exports or a reduction in imports must be to a country's advantage. M. Mauroy did not explain precisely how European agriculture's duty to the Third World has been fulfilled by the restrictions imposed under the Common Agricultural Policy on low-cost agricultural exports from developing countries, or for that matter by driving down the world price of sugar, on which some of these countries are heavily dependent, through sales of high-cost Community surpluses.

More commonly it is manufacturing, rather than agriculture, which is assigned a leading role. Such a casting exercise, though of a modest kind, was performed in an interview given last year by Mr Alfred Eckes, the then Chairman of the US International Trade Commission which advises the President on applications from American industries for protection against imports. Mr Eckes spoke of the need for older US industries to modernize, and added:

I really don't believe, myself, that this nation is going to become a nation of hamburger stands, Chinese restaurants, laundries, banks and computer operators. I think we have to have some sort of manufacturing sector.[3]

For Mr Eckes, it is the manifest destiny of Americans to manufacture. However, different forms of soap operatics often go together, and his apparent distaste for the service sector is, I suspect, influenced by structure snobbery as well.

Structure snobbery entails the remarkably widespread belief that winners and also-rans can be identified within a country's economy – that is, activities which are to be desired and favoured for what they are, and others which, if not positively undesirable, can be seen to be lacking in dynamism or otherwise less worthy of esteem. As to which activities fall into what category, it is simply taken for granted that well informed observers – politicians, civil servants, businessmen, scientists – can easily judge this. A widespread variant of structure snobbery is the idea that it is both demeaning and bad policy for a country to export raw materials and import manufactures. Why is it considered demeaning? Because this was supposedly the role that the former imperial powers imposed upon their colonies. Why is it thought to be bad policy? Partly because manufacturing is perceived as inherently a more rewarding form of economic activity than agriculture or mining, but mainly – and here again there is a close link with traditional mercantilism – because it is thought to be advantageous for a country to export products in more finished rather than less finished form, since this will improve its balance of payments and create employment.

Given this perception, one possible line of policy for governments is to forbid or discourage exports of raw materials. History gives many examples of this practice. Here is one from the early part of the reign of Frederick the Great, following his acquisition of Silesia in the 1740s:

Formerly fine linen yarn from Silesia had been sent to Holland to be bleached. Now the export of yarn was prohibited. The only exception to this rule was that yarn might be sent to Bohemia to be woven provided that it was eventually sent back to Silesia to be bleached.[4]

One present-day counterpart to eighteenth-century linen yarn is timber. For instance, the government of Indonesia has forbidden the export of logs, in order to ensure that timber is exported only in sawn form; and similarly, exports of logs are largely banned from the US federal lands west of the 100th meridian, while a number of individual states within the US have laws which ban the export of logs from timber grown on state lands. Again, although as we shall see other motives are present in this case, there are restrictions on the export from the US of crude petroleum: in particular, there is a ban on exports of Alaskan oil, for which ready markets exist in Japan. In a recent defence of this latter restriction, a senior Democratic member of the House of Representatives, Congressman John Dingell, said that he was 'totally opposed to export of oil to Japan', for a 'very simple' reason, namely:

> We now occupy the position of a colony with Japan: we send them raw materials and they send us finished products ... That's a very clever way of increasing Japanese prosperity at the expense of the United States.[5]

Here the Congressman was unconsciously echoing a line of argument which had been used some months earlier in a speech by the Prime Minister of Malaysia, Dr Mahathir, who asserted that trade flows between Malaysia and Japan conformed to 'the classic pattern of economic colonialism'.[6] Soap operatics knows no frontiers, while the view of trade relationships taken by these eminent political figures was a familiar one in the seventeenth century.[7]

Essentialist soap operatics

In the cases I have just quoted, exports of raw materials are
discouraged largely in order to make way for something
better. But other situations can be found where such
exports are subject to control and even prohibition, not on
the grounds that they are inferior or unrewarding products,
but because on the contrary they are too precious to be
made freely available to foreigners. In these situations, both
structure snobbery and the traditional mercantilist concern
for improving the balance of trade are set aside. The third
form of soap operatics, namely *essentialism*, has come into
operation. According to this simple-minded doctrine, the
outputs and activities of an economic system can usefully
be divided into two broad categories, essential and inessential, the distinction between which must be apparent to any
experienced person. The purpose of export restrictions is to
reserve essential products for home consumption.

In this connection, essentialists are strongly attracted to
energy products. Thus in Australia, for example, 'petroleum exports are limited to ensure that the requirements
of the domestic market are satisfied'.[8] The US restrictions
on the export of crude petroleum, some of which go back to
the 1920s, have a similar rationale: domestic consumers'
needs come first. In Canada, 'All exports of energy (except
coal) must be approved by the Federal Government'; and
in the case of natural gas, the federal National Energy
Board 'will license gas exports only if there is a demonstrated surplus of "reasonably foreseeable Canadian
requirements"'.[9] Moreover, in the case of Canadian natural
gas it is not only the federal government that licenses
exports: similar restrictions have been operated for almost
40 years by the provincial government of Alberta, where
the natural gas deposits are largely found. The Alberta
Conservation Board estimates likely 'requirements' of
natural gas within the province over a 25–30 year period;
compares these figures with estimated reserves both proved

and possible; and determines the exportable surplus, including exports to the rest of Canada, on the basis of this comparison. Long term projections of reserves and home demand also form the basis of the export licensing system applied to coal by the government of the Republic of South Africa. The object in such cases is to conserve non-renewable resources for essential domestic uses into the indefinite future.

What about North Sea oil and gas? What has been the official British attitude to these issues? Policy under successive governments, here as in other areas, betrays clearly the influence of DIYE; but the influence is stronger in gas than in oil. It is true that in both cases the government has extensive powers of control over the disposal of production. Both oil and gas have to be landed in the UK, though this requirement can be waived in special circumstances; and exports of crude oil are subject to licence, which would no doubt be true of gas also if the question of exporting should ever become a serious one. To this extent both products are treated in the same way; and this treatment distinguishes them from most other forms of output – for after all, an export licence is not regarded as necessary for buses or turbine generators or cashmere sweaters.

Nevertheless, oil and gas have been treated differently. Governments of both parties have flirted now and then with the idea of imposing restrictions, formal or informal, on exports of crude oil; but for the past five years at least, and very largely before that, producers have been free to choose their own markets and destinations. In gas, by contrast, essentialism has reigned supreme, ever since the first discoveries were made in the Southern Basin of the North Sea some 20 years ago, and regardless of which party has been in power. One aspect of this is that exports of gas, though not actually impermissible under the relevant legislation, have been deliberately ruled out as a possibility. When the present Chancellor of the Exchequer, Nigel

Lawson, became Secretary of State for Energy in 1981, it crossed my mind that as a supposedly market-oriented minister he might change this state of affairs; but on balance I thought it unlikely. It was therefore with surprise that I saw a headline in *The Times* on 11 February 1982 which read: 'Lawson ready to consider exports of North Sea gas'. But reading on, I saw that essentialism was still firmly in place: reporting Lawson's words, the article said: 'Sales abroad would be considered . . . only if sufficient new discoveries were made.' This remains the official British government position, in which it is strongly supported by the British Gas Corporation.

It is not only in relation to energy products that governments make use of export restrictions on largely essentialist grounds. Thus in 1974, in face of a steep rise in world prices, the US government imposed a ban on the export of soya beans, which are a major export commodity; and although in the American case this measure proved temporary and has not since been reintroduced, the government of Brazil, another leading exporter of soya beans, has made regular use of export controls. Similarly, the government of India resorts to export licensing of tea when world prices are considered high. In the European Community, exports of scrap metal are subject to licence; and in early 1985, when world prices of ferrous scrap rose sharply, there was strong pressure from steel producers for export restrictions to be imposed.

Micawber's dichotomy and unreflecting centralism

Essentialism, by the way, illustrates a chronic bias in the DIYE perception of choices and alternatives. The bias is towards the dramatic, and a leading example of it is Charles Dickens's Mr Micawber, when he laid down the following justly famous socioeconomic proposition:

Annual income twenty pounds, annual expenditure nineteen pounds nineteen and six, result happiness. Annual income twenty pounds, annual expenditure twenty pounds ought and six, result misery.

The argument here would not impress my colleague Mr MacQuedy, who would point out with justice that the difference between these two alleged extremes was only one-eighth of one per cent each way. This illustrates a characteristic difference between do-it-yourself economics, which is apt to see the world in terms of sharp contrasts, switches and discontinuities, and the orthodox economists' picture of reality which emphasizes – some would say overemphasizes – continuity and incremental changes.

Here is a recent high-level example of Micawber's dichotomy, embodying the tacit assumption that only extreme outcomes are possible. At the Conservative Party Conference of October 1984 the Secretary of State for Energy, Peter Walker, made the following assessment of the possible consequences of allowing coal to be freely imported into Britain.

We could import a lot of cheap coal at certain times. That could undermine our industry and we could close all of our pits. Then we would become very dependent upon that imported cheap coal – and when we did so, it would no longer be cheap.[10]

For Mr Walker, there are two stark and widely separated alternatives. Either 'we' keep out coal imports, and have a coal industry to call our own, or we permit imports at the risk of having no such industry. The numerous intermediate possibilities are swept aside, including the possibility that coal imports would displace a limited and varying amount of especially high-cost domestic coal. Also underlying Mr Walker's argument, I think, is a presumption that imports are supplied by a small group of foreign agencies who are in a position to exert monopoly power. I shall return to this common presumption in my next lecture.

In what way does essentialism mean taking Mr Micawber's side in the debate? Because on this view there is for essentials a narrow margin only between a situation in which supplies fall short of needs and one in which they exceed them. In the former case there is scarcity, which is a serious matter. In the latter case, there is a surplus; and some or even all of this surplus can then legitimately be sold to foreigners, because it is worth relatively little at home.

Note that if this is indeed a full and accurate description of the situation, then the prices of essential products or services are liable to fluctuate widely. In times of scarcity they will be pushed up, perhaps almost indefinitely, without having much effect except to impoverish consumers because essential requirements have to be met pretty well regardless of cost. In times of surplus they will fall, and again demand will not respond much. Price movements in these circumstances would have little impact on sales, but would involve substantial transfers of income from one group within the community to another. Thus from an essentialist point of view free markets appear as rather arbitrary and inefficient mechanisms for allocating supplies, at any rate in the short run; and it is natural to conclude that this places on governments the responsibility for assuring that essential demands are met and sharp price changes avoided.

The use of export restrictions, which is by no means confined to energy products, is of course only one means of giving effect to the idea that governments must take direct administrative measures to ensure that essential needs come first. Just as regulations can favour domestic consumers as against foreigners, so they can be used to discriminate among domestic consumers themselves. Such measures can be short-term or more permanent. A leading example of the latter is provided by the British Gas Corporation, in whose strategic thinking a clear line is drawn between 'premium' and 'non-premium' uses of gas. To quote some official words on the subject, which remain as pertinent now as when they were written under a Labour government in 1978:

> The policy of British Gas, agreed with the Government, is to sell gas in the markets where its particular qualities give it a premium value (domestic usage, other space heating and industrial processes where a high grade fuel is required). However, premium demand fluctuates widely between summer and winter and so, to operate economically as well as to maintain operational flexibility and security of supply, British Gas sells a limited amount of gas in non-premium markets on an interruptible basis.[11]

It can be seen that in their view of domestic markets, as well as in their hostility to exports, the British Gas Corporation and successive British governments have been consistently guided by essentialist ideas. Here there is also a link with a further aspect of DIYE, which I call *unreflecting centralism*. One form of this is a readiness to assume that decisions have to be taken by governments, as in the case of gas where it is the government or its chosen agents who determine what is premium and what is not.

An orthodox criterion: willingness to pay at the margin

Let me use this particular aspect of British energy policy as the occasion for beginning to unveil the orthodox alternative. When uses of gas are designated as premium or non-premium, it has to be asked: What is the basis of this distinction, and who is to judge which is which? I have actually heard it suggested at a high level that the difference between the two categories is not economic, but thermal or physical, so that for instance it is simply in the nature of things that gas, as a premium fuel, should not be put to such an unworthy low-grade use as raising steam to generate electricity in power stations. But in Ireland and Bangladesh for example, where alternative fuels are relatively much more costly than in Britain, gas *is* used as a fuel for power stations. Why should this be ruled out? Surely the test must be an economic one, which makes allowance for different circumstances, rather than one of techno-aesthetic intuition? And once it is admitted that the question of the best pattern of use is economic, it is unnecessary to bring in such soap-operatic categories as premium and non-premium or essential and non-essential. We can use a simple alternative approach.

It was a character in an Oscar Wilde play who remarked that a cynic is a man who knows the price of everything and the value of nothing. This may be an odd definition of a cynic, but it is not an unfair caricature of an orthodox economist such as my colleague Mr MacQuedy. For him, it is natural to ask how the value of something could be determined, except by reference to the price that people reveal themselves as being prepared to pay for it. *Prima facie* at least, what is useful or valuable can be identified only on the basis of demonstrated *willingness to pay*.

This does not make Mr MacQuedy a crude materialist or a heartless monster: the real point that he is making can be illustrated with another energy-related example. At the time of the second oil crisis of 1979–80, a suggestion was made by the UK Road Haulage Association that the British government should adopt a new policy in relation to petroleum, and 'consider reducing or abandoning its use for non-transport purposes'.[12] The argument was twofold: first, that other users of oil could get by without it, albeit in some cases with difficulty, while transport could not; and second, that transport was an essential service. Although British Gas Corporation terminology was not actually used, in effect transport was identified as the only premium use for oil.

Suppose that a government accepted this line of argument. What would it then do? It could issue regulations forbidding the use of petroleum products for certain specified purposes. It could go further, by allowing petroleum products to be bought only under licence, and arranging that over time these licences to buy were increasingly issued only for transport uses.

Consider the case where there is a comprehensive licensing system, which establishes a particular allocation or pattern of usage for oil – an allocation which has been decided centrally, according to the government's assessment of priorities. Is there any way of deciding whether a better allocation is possible? Yes, there is. If a particular user X found it worth while to buy and use some extra tons of oil at the going price, and if at the same time another consumer Y found it worth while to sell that same amount, then both would be better off, in their own estimation at least, if the exchange between them took place. Even within the constraints of an allocation system, the exchange could take place if Y was allowed to sell to X his licence to buy that amount. Since no one else would be made worse off by such private transactions, the new allocation can be judged, and would be judged by Mr MacQuedy and me, to be better than the initial one. Moreover, it would still be judged better even if it so happened that X did not use this extra amount for transport, while Y would have used it for transport if the transaction had not taken place. The fact that some minister or high-level commmittee has decided that one use is essential, premium or high priority, while another use is inessential, non-premium or low priority, is beside the point. The point is that the new allocation, based on demonstrated willingness to pay, makes a given amount of oil more valuable than it was before. The same would apply to gas, or to any other product for which for some reason a system of rationing, formal or informal, short-term or long-term, had been introduced.

At this point I need to introduce a key phrase from the

technical vocabulary of economics. Note that in this
hypothetical example of exchange, there is no question of Y
having to give up all use of the product in question, nor of
X being a non-consumer before the deal is made. These are
not all-or-nothing Micawberist decisions. In the new
situation as compared with the old one, X buys and uses
rather more, and Y rather less. It can therefore be said of
this transaction – and the same applies to most transactions
within an economic system – that it takes place *at the margin*.
Hence the criterion which orthodox economics suggests, in
this case and more generally, is not simply that of
willingness to pay: it is willingness to pay at the margin.

Individualism as a principle

In my examples, willingness to pay is expressed by
individual agents within the economic system – people,
households, businesses or non-profit-making organizations.
For Mr MacQuedy, it is their judgement as to what is
valuable, guided by their conception of their own interests,
that should decide the pattern of use, rather than the
judgement of ministers and government officials. In this
sense, orthodox economics is *individualist*. Situations and
measures are judged in terms of their effects on the welfare
of individuals, whose preferences are made effective
through market transactions by virtue of demonstrated
willingness to pay.

   Now it may be objected, quite reasonably, that this
pro-market, anti-soap opera case, as set out in the context
of the examples I have just given, depends on the
assumption that individual buyers and sellers are good
judges of their own interests. If not, then the mere fact that
a voluntary exchange makes both parties to it better off in
their own estimation does not establish that the exchange
would lead to a genuine improvement. A sceptical person
could point out that it is easy to think of lawful purchases

by individuals – of alcohol and tobacco, for instance – which might be better not made; that there are important areas of choice, such as health care, where consumers are often neither well informed nor dispassionate; and that people, and even businesses, may be swayed by advertising and other persuasive influences to act in ways that do not reflect their best interests.

None of these possibilities is denied by Mr MacQuedy. Briefly, his response is as follows. First, it is certainly the case that individuals are not always or necessarily good judges of where their interests lie. However, there are wide areas of economic life within which they are at any rate more competent to judge them than an official agency could be. In the case of oil, for example, it is a reasonable presumption that individual users, such as the members of the British Road Haulage Association, can judge better than government departments how best to lay out their own money to serve their own ends. Second, voluntary transactions between individuals help them to acquire knowledge and experience that make them better judges of their interests. In this connection, as in others, advertising can serve a useful function. Third, though this takes us beyond the domain of economic calculations of gain and loss, considerations of individual liberty are involved. Lastly, these are admittedly difficult issues. All the more reason, therefore, not to decide them with reference to the arbitrary labels and categories of economic soap opera.

Let me add that MacQuedy's criterion of individual willingness to pay at the margin is not to be insisted on in all conceivable circumstances. As short-term expedients particularly, administrative measures have their uses. In a period of drought a prohibition on washing cars may be justified, the more so if water supplies are not metered. If power supplies have to be reduced in an emergency, it makes good sense to give priority to hospitals, without asking each hospital administrator how much he would be prepared to pay in order to avoid being cut off. All that orthodoxy suggests is that the criterion should be relied on as a general rule, and extended as widely as is practicable.

Markets, rationing and justice

A frequent objection to relying on markets is that it makes for injustice. It is argued that 'rationing by the purse' causes poor consumers to be squeezed out, and that they should be guaranteed minimum supplies of essentials at reasonable prices. Let me comment on this, both with reference to energy examples and more generally.

In the first place, it is worth noting that questions of inequality and poverty need not be involved at all. Administrative modes of allocation are not necessarily, or even usually, designed to benefit the poor. Thus the British Gas Corporation's policy of giving preference to so-called 'premium' users does not involve a means test; and the reasons why most licences to operate in the UK sector of the North Sea are not auctioned have nothing to do with official concern about poverty. There is nothing surprising or improper about this. Indeed, it is arguable that in these and many other cases considerations of poverty are irrelevant. Suppose for example that petrol (gasoline) is rationed through the issue of coupons. In so far as the interests of the poor are to count, the right course of action would be to allocate coupons to demonstrably poor people, whether or not they are owners of motor vehicles, and allow them to sell any coupons they wish for the best prices they can get. But most vehicle owners would regard this as grossly unfair; and so far as I know, all past schemes of petrol rationing in every country have assigned ration coupons exclusively to vehicle owners and operators. This illustrates a point to which I shall return, namely that poverty and inequality are not the only aspects of economic justice that governments have to consider.

The argument that the interests of the poor should be

protected through special low-cost provision is applied mainly to a limited range of items that are viewed as essential, and which enter into every one's consumption. The kinds of purchases that are usually listed are food, clothing, shelter and certain energy products used by households. But in relation to these, a point to bear in mind is that with one significant exception, namely subsidized public housing, such special low-cost allocation schemes are not widely used or officially favoured in economically developed democratic countries. In Britain, governments of both parties have taken the view that the problems of poverty and economic inequality should be dealt with more directly – the problem of poverty through cash transfers within the social security system, and that of inequality through the system of taxation as well as social security. Manipulating the prices of basic goods and services for these purposes is frowned on. Here is a statement of this rather market-oriented philosophy, taken from the 1978 White Paper on the UK nationalized industries which was issued by the last Labour government:

> The Government intends that the nationalized industries will not be forced into deficits by restraints on their prices. When help has to be given to poorer members of the community it will be given primarily through the social security and taxation system, and not by subsidising nationalized industry prices.[13]

Thus it is a mistake to think that in the debate between orthodoxy and common sense economics the issues chiefly involved are those of poverty and inequality. The question of who will lose and who will gain from particular policies, and how these gains and losses should be weighed, is always pertinent. But there is no presumption that the actual measures taken by present-day governments on the basis of soap operatic or other DIYE criteria have either the intention or the effect of helping the poor.

Regulations versus markets

In so far as individual willingness to pay at the margin is taken as a guide to action, administrative restrictions on the freedom to buy and sell are put in question; and so also is any form of administrative rationing – whether through coupons, permits, licences or queues. In my example, the most valuable use for oil could be achieved, without resort to licences or restrictions, largely by allowing prices to act as a rationing device. If, however, there was some particular reason for issuing licences, much the same allocation could be brought about by putting the licences up to auction. In any case, whether they have been auctioned or not, allowing licences to be freely bought or sold would keep open opportunities for improving whatever the allocation happened to be.

It is easy to think of real-life situations in which it would be possible to put greater reliance on the test of individual willingness to pay. Should British Gas be instructed to cease discriminating between different categories of consumer? Why not assign all licences for oil companies to operate in the North Sea on the basis of sealed bid auctions, instead of just a few as at present? Given that milk quotas have been imposed on British dairy farmers under European Community regulations, is there scope for enabling these quotas to be freely bought and sold? Could housing problems be eased by phasing out rent controls, and allowing council tenants the right to sell their own leases? These and similar questions are provoked by the kind of argument that I have been sketching out. The orthodox economic approach does not in itself provide ready-made definitive answers for them. It offers a guiding principle – the principle being that markets should be enabled to function effectively, so that scarce resources will be put to their most productive use. Orthodox economics is, in a word, market-oriented; and a not entirely respectful descriptive term coined by an economist friend and former colleague of mine, Paul Streeten, can be applied to Mr MacQuedy and me: we are 'price mechanists'.

Outside the rather disorderly ranks of the economics profession, this is not a popular creed. It is rare to find a government that is prepared to auction licences and quotas or allow them to be freely tradable. Public opinion often supports governments in this, and is in general suspicious of the idea that markets should be allowed to operate freely. In the next two lectures also, I shall be concerned with issues on which Mr MacQuedy and I are conscious of being very much in a minority.

Notes

1 P.J.D. Wiles, *Communist International Economics*, Oxford, Blackwell, 1968.
2 *The Times*, 12 December 1983.
3 *Financial Times*, 17 May 1984.
4 W.O. Henderson, *Studies in the Economic Policy of Frederick the Great*, London, Frank Cass & Co. Ltd , 1963, p. 142.
5 *Inside Energy*, 13 May 1985.
6 *Financial Times*, 28 August 1984.
7 Actually Mr Eckes shared these worries: he described the US trade relationship with Japan, Korea and Taiwan as 'reminiscent of the colonial trade pattern this country had with Great Britain in the 18th century'.
8 International Energy Agency, *Energy Policies and Programmes of IEA Countries: 1984 Review*, Paris, OECD, 1985, p. 152.
9 *Ibid.*, p. 210.
10 *The Economist*, 26 January 1985.
11 *Development of the Oil and Gas Resources of the United Kingdom*, London, HMSO, 1978, p. 21.
12 *The Times*, 19 February 1980.
13 *The Nationalised Industries*, Cmnd 7131, London, HMSO, 1978.

3

NEEDS, CENTRALISM AND AUTARCHY

. . . I have made this basic decision: In allocating the products of America's farms between markets abroad and those in the United States, we must put the American consumer first.

Therefore, I have decided that a new system for export controls on food products is needed . . . (Richard Nixon, when President of the United States, 'Address to the Nation Announcing Price Control Measures', 13 June 1973)

In this lecture I shall enlarge on the contrast between the ideas and beliefs of do-it-yourself economics – DIYE for short – and those of economic orthodoxy. In particular, I shall discuss some oversimplified but influential notions concerning the role of governments in relation to supposed national needs.

Twin aspects of unreflecting centralism

I want to consider first the aspect of DIYE which I have called unreflecting centralism. It has two mutually supporting elements. One, which I have referred to already, is the disposition to assume that outcomes have to be planned and decided by governments. The second is the tendency to think of governments and states as the principal, or even the only, actors on the economic scene, and to attribute to them roles and functions which are not necessarily theirs.

A good example of this tendency appeared in a speech which I had the pleasure of hearing in Brussels last year by the present Prime Minister of the Republic of Ireland, Dr Garret FitzGerald. Interestingly, Dr FitzGerald is one of two prime ministers within the European Community who count as professional economists, the other being the Prime Minister of Greece, Dr Andreas Papandreou. In his speech, he described himself engagingly as 'an economist on leave'. Nevertheless, in reviewing the problems of the Community, he advanced a prize specimen of unreflecting centralism.

For Dr FitzGerald there are two economic superpowers, the United States and Japan, and, he argued:

> attempts to compete on an equal basis in the economic sphere with these super-powers by independent, individual action, are quite simply bound to fail.[1]

The moral drawn by Dr FitzGerald, in common with many other influential people, is that the governments of the European Community must take concerted action to strengthen the competitive position of the Community as a whole *vis-à-vis* the United States and Japan.

This argument assumes that competition in the markets of the world is between states, and that only large states can successfully engage in it. Both propositions are false. Competition is largely between a multitude of business enterprises of all kinds, over a wide range of specific products and markets. It is true that governments can influence the outcome of the competitive process in various ways, and that particular business enterprises can be owned or backed by governments. But even when this is allowed for, it is not states that are generally the sole or the principal parties to the vast array of individual transactions around the world in which the competitive process takes shape.

As to large states being necessarily more successful on the contemporary economic scene, this notion is hard to reconcile with the fact that in Europe it is two small countries, Sweden and Switzerland, which by conventional tests are possibly the most economically advanced. The products of Swedish and Swiss enterprises have for decades competed successfully on world markets, without benefit of concerted transnational 'industrial strategies' of the kind that are now so favoured in official and business circles within the European Community. If we look outside Europe, and at the growth of income per head and of exports to world markets, the outstanding success stories of the past two decades are to be found among the developing countries of east and south-east Asia. Three of the most successful of these, Hong Kong, Singapore and Taiwan, are small, while none of the group is very large. In any case, it is not the governments of these countries, through concerted action among themselves, that have achieved rapidly increasing shares in expanding world markets. This has been the work of individual enterprises – helped, it should be said, by government policies which have provided an environment in which enterprises could grow and flourish, but which have not been based on the mistaken assumption that competition on world markets is largely between states.

Let me quote another official instance of unreflecting centralism, which will take us back into energy policy. A few years ago, in an interesting letter to *The Times* about the United Kingdom nuclear power programme, a former senior British government official, Peter Vinter, observed that: 'As a nation we have not yet succeeded in setting up an effective nuclear reactor construction company'.[2] I think his point is a fair one, and perhaps he would say the same today. But why should it be the collective responsibility of 'we as a nation' to establish a nuclear reactor construction company? Why should such a company, if indeed there is a place for it, not emerge from the impersonal competitive selection process of markets, without benefit of high-level official committees?

The history of British nuclear power programmes over the past 30 years provides a depressing example of unreflecting centralism in action – stoutly reinforced, I may add, by other forms of DIYE. One aspect of this centralism is the idea, which has been embraced by successive British governments of both parties, that a choice has to be made at Cabinet level of one particular reactor system for future nuclear power stations in Britain. Here for instance is David Howell giving evidence to a House of Commons Select Committee in 1980, when he was Secretary of State for Energy under Mrs Thatcher:

> . . . we must develop a sound thermal reactor strategy . . . we are virtually the only major industrialised country without a chosen reactor system available for series ordering . . . we cannot continue to run two systems indefinitely . . .[3]

Note that here again it is 'we as a nation', with Her Majesty's Government as agent, that has to decide these things. In Mr Howell's world, in the world of his predecessors and his successors and their official advisers, no other practical possibility exists. It has been taken for granted, whatever the party in office, that the Secretary of State for Energy, or indeed the Cabinet itself, must determine the size of the nuclear power programme, the choice of reactor, and the appropriate structure for the nuclear industry.

But in fact, there are other ways of handling these issues. A few years ago an interesting article made me aware of how nuclear power had developed in Switzerland.[4] The title of the article, significantly, was 'How Switzerland has Benefited from the Market Approach'. At the time when it appeared, there were four nuclear reactors in operation within Switzerland, at three different power stations. The choice of reactors, as of other systems and equipment in the stations, was made not by the federal government but by the individual utilities concerned, which are small by British standards since the Swiss electricity supply industry is much more decentralized. Two different reactor systems have been chosen and are in operation. According to the article 'The four operating nuclear units were built in remarkably good time and within their original cost budget' – an achievement, I might add, which is in marked contrast with British results over the past two decades. As to operating performance, a recent comparative table shows the load factors achieved around the world by 232 nuclear reactors. Taking cumulative performance over the whole operating lives of these reactors, the best of the Swiss quartet was ranked third out of the 232, while the worst was placed at 29th.[5]

Essentialism at the national level

One reason for centralism, which applies in energy policy and a number of other fields, is the uncritical acceptance of essentialist ideas. In the case of energy, each country is perceived as having needs which must be met, and each national government as having an inescapable responsibility to anticipate and provide for these needs. In the more rustic treatments of these questions, reference is made to a possible 'energy gap' which the government has to ensure is bridged. Even in more sophisticated official presentations, governments usually appear as indispensable providers. Here again is David Howell, from his period as Secretary of State for Energy:

> The Government, in my view, must ensure that we have enough energy in the future to heat our homes and to power our industries. Failure to achieve this could mean lower living standards for us all and a very severe constraint on our society.[6]

So essentialism leads naturally to unreflecting centralism. Also here in its place on the DIYE stage is Micawber's dichotomy: either we-as-a-nation have enough energy, or we do not. But who is to say how much is enough? You will search in vain in official White Papers and statistical publications for figures showing national energy needs, for the simple reason that the concept can be neither defined nor measured. If you ask some one who uses the term what are the current or prospective energy needs of the United Kingdom, the only answer you will get is a figure which relates to *demand* – in other words, to actual or prospective purchases of energy products. Demand is identified with needs, for no better reason than that energy, like food, is cast in the soap opera script as essential.

This takes no account of the fact that not all purchases of a product or service are of equal value to those who make them. For pretty well any consumer, of energy or anything else, a 10 per cent enforced cut in purchases and usage would bring about a loss in welfare more than five times as great as a reduction of 2 per cent. To class all energy purchases indiscriminately as essential is to miss the point that most transactions take place at the margin; and at the margin energy products, like other products, are generally valued by people and by businesses at the prices which they show themselves as willing to pay for them.

Clear evidence of this is that purchases of energy respond to changes in relative prices, which they would not if they were literally requirements that had to be met. Between 1973 and 1983 the real national product of the United Kingdom – in other words, the total output of goods and services – rose by something like 10 per cent. If there were indeed national requirements for energy in any literal sense, these would no doubt have risen somewhat in response. But over these ten years estimated inland energy consumption actually fell, by more than 10 per cent. This of course was not because the government failed in its supposed duty as provider, but largely because energy prices rose considerably in relation to other prices. The pattern of expenditure changed accordingly, reflecting individual decisions based on willingness to pay.

At this point I fancy I hear the groans from some of my professional colleagues. Henderson, they are saying, is wasting the Reith Lectures labouring points which are familiar to every first year economics student, and are not important anyway. Well, as to importance, I shall let the evidence that I have presented, and will present, speak for itself. As to familiarity, I would make two responses to the critics: first, they are badly out of touch with first year economics students; and second, they should note that intuitive economic ideas have cast their spell not only on our eminent professional colleague Dr FitzGerald, but also on Mr Howell, who himself has a first class degree in economics.

The goal of autarchy

Both in the energy field and elsewhere, essentialist ideas lend support to another aspect of DIYE, namely the belief that *autarchy*, or national self-sufficiency, is an important goal, especially for the goods and services that have been labelled as essential. Here is a recent illustration from the European Commission in Brussels. A newspaper report in the summer of 1985 bore the heading 'EEC grain could be converted to plastics' – an intriguing gloss on the supposed 'vocation' of European Community agriculture, which I referred to in my last lecture. In this article the Commissioner for Industry, Karl Heinz Narjes, was quoted as saying that:

> Current Commission policy seeks to encourage food self-sufficiency in developing countries as the only reliable long-term solution to their needs.[7]

Here again Micawberism is with us – either a country is

self-sufficient or it is not – while centralism is also implied, since it is governments alone which can make sure that self-sufficiency is achieved.

The idea that it is important for developing countries to become self-sufficient in food is widely and uncritically accepted, not just in Brussels; but from the orthodox economic standpoint it is without foundation. There is no magic accession of strength that a country derives from reducing imports of food to zero or a little less, whether for individual commodities or across the whole range. Hong Kong has developed over the past three decades as rapidly perhaps as any country in history. It is at present dependent on imports for approximately seven-eighths of its food consumption. There is no reason to suppose that it would have gained in the past, or would gain in the future, from deliberate official attempts to bring down this ratio, while 100 per cent self-sufficiency would be absurdly costly. Neither in Hong Kong nor anywhere else does it make sense to specify as an aim of policy, on the basis of soap operatic intuition alone, a particular ratio of domestic production to total consumption. This generalization applies to all products, including food, and to all countries whether rich or poor.

Security within the national fortress?

For some people, this statement of orthodox economic doctrine may appear too unqualified, since it fails to mention explicitly security of supply. Often though not always, the case for self-sufficiency is argued with reference to a country's need to ensure security by minimizing dependence on foreign sources. The outside world is seen at best as unreliable and subject to instability, at worst as actively hostile. From this fortress mentality standpoint, autarchy appears to be common prudence. Two sets of measures then suggest themselves: one is to build up domestic production of essentials so as to reduce imports to a minimum; the other is to restrict exports, so as to ensure that domestic supplies are available for domestic use.

Not surprisingly, the tendency to think in these terms has been strengthened in recent years by developments on international energy markets, and in particular by the two oil crises of 1973–4 and 1979–80. Here for example is the then President of the United States, Richard Nixon, in an Address to the Nation in November 1973, launching the programme known as Project Independence:

> Let us set as our national goal . . . that by the end of this decade we will have developed the potential to meet our own energy needs without depending on any foreign sources.[8]

Again, the American Energy Security Act of 1980 laid down a specific programme for reducing dependence on imported oil, through the production of 'at least 500,000 barrels of crude oil per day of synthetic fuel by 1987'.[9] Also in 1980, following the second oil crisis, the then (Liberal) government of Canada adopted a comprehensive National Energy Program. In the official document setting out the Program, one of the 'three precepts for federal action' underlying it was stated as being to:

> . . . establish the basis for Canadians to seize control of their own energy future through security of supply and ultimate independence of the world market.[10]

In the British case, official policy towards North Sea oil was dominated in its early phase, under governments of both parties, by the wish to achieve self-sufficiency as soon as possible. Once this goal was within sight, successive governments flirted with the notion of a 'depletion policy', which by controlling the rate of North Sea development would ensure that something reasonably close to self-sufficency would be maintained for longer than would otherwise be the case. In July 1980 Mr Howell actually announced such a policy; and he referred in particular to action that would be taken 'to deter some oil production from the 1980s'.[11]

What is the orthodox economic response to these arguments, and to the policies based on them? Mr MacQuedy would agree that the question of security of supply has to be faced, by governments as well as by other agents within an economy, and that it may well be worth while to incur some extra cost at the margin to achieve a higher degree of security. But he does not share the fortress mentality, nor does he think much of the kinds of autarchic measures that are prompted by it.

One reason for scepticism is the eventual fate of the sort of energy policies that I have mentioned, which were confidently launched with the object of achieving energy security by reducing dependence on imports and on world markets. Who now remembers Project Independence? In 1973, the year in which it was launched with such fanfare, the estimated share of United States energy consumption supplied by domestic sources was 85 per cent. In 1980, when the authors of Project Independence had envisaged that it would be approaching 100 per cent, it was in fact 86 per cent. As for the 1980 US synthetic fuel target, of 500,000 barrels of oil equivalent per day by 1987, the likely outcome in that year is something much lower, possibly 10–15,000 barrels per day; and this is fortunate, because if the target had been reached the costs involved would have been inordinately high. The Canadian National Energy Program of 1980 no longer exists as such; and the central feature of it which I quoted, namely the aim of isolating Canada from world energy markets, has been abandoned. In all these cases centralized official strategies soon proved to be unrealistic and unworkable. Meanwhile the modest British depletion policy, also of 1980, has long since been quietly laid to rest.

It is true that such failures and reversals of policy are partly due to the fact that governments, like individuals, can easily misjudge the future course of events. But even if economic change were more predictable, there would remain basic objections from the orthodox economic point of view to the kinds of autarchic policies which are associated with essentialism and the fortress mentality.

In particular, it is wrong to think of security of supply in essentialist terms. Security of supply is not a separate dimension of choice: it is one of the economic aspects. Like other features of the quality of a purchase, such as reliability in service, it has a value; and the best indication of this value is willingness to pay at the margin. This can easily be seen in those markets where buyers are offered a free choice between interruptible and non-interruptible supply contracts; and, more generally, considerations of security affect decisions about how far ahead to make commitments, and what sort of contracts to sign. Just as there are no precisely defined national needs that have to be met regardless of cost, so there are no overriding requirements for uninterrupted supply which can be identified in central bureaucracies and used as a basis for policies.

Exports, willingness to pay and international markets

To see where this argument leads, let us consider export prohibitions. According to do-it-yourself economics, these are called for in the case of products that are both essential and scarce. British policies toward North Sea oil and gas provide an illustration. Governments have consistently ruled out exports of gas, on the grounds that estimated reserves are too limited: in this case, scarcity is viewed as chronic. By contrast, exports of crude oil are generally unrestricted though subject to licence; it is clear, however, that freedom to export is liable to be curtailed in periods of shortage. Just before the general election of 1979 the then

Secretary of State for Energy, Tony Benn, was reported as having reacted to news that an oil company operating in the North Sea 'had seriously considered cutting back on supplies in Britain and selling the surplus at higher prices in Europe'. His reaction was:

> to ask the chairmen of all the major oil companies operating here to give him their personal assurances that they are not taking advantage of the general oil shortage in this way.[12]

Shortly afterwards it was reported of Mr Benn's Conservative successor, David Howell, that he had 'started a discreet but forceful squeeze on North Sea oil companies to keep more of their production at home'.[13] The squeeze had to be discreet, since formal restrictions might well have been – and would still be – hard to reconcile with obligations which Britain has assumed as a member both of the European Community and of the International Energy Agency. But it could nevertheless be forceful, since an oil company that failed to respond might prejudice its chances of success in the next round of applications for North Sea licences. The situation has not changed since those early days of Mrs Thatcher's prime ministership. If another oil crisis arose, ways would probably be found, whatever government was in power, to safeguard the principle laid down by Mr Howell in a speech of June 1979, that 'the interests of British consumers must come first'.[14]

Note that in such cases as oil and gas it is considered irrelevant that exports might command a higher price than domestic sales: prohibitions should still apply. Indeed, Hamish Gray, who at the time was (Conservative) Minister of State at the Department of Energy, was reported a few years ago as having committed himself, while speaking of a particular North Sea gas field, to the remarkable statement that 'Britain would not consider selling its share of the Statfjord gas whatever price a foreign buyer might offer'.[15]

This conception of national interest is not shared by Mr

MacQuedy. For him, the test of willingness to pay at the margin does not cease to hold good just because national frontiers are involved. How much particular exports are worth to the economy depends on the value of the imports for which they can be exchanged, which in turn depends on how much foreigners are prepared to pay for them. If prices rise and there is pressure on supplies in world markets, why should domestic consumers of the product concerned be given unlimited preference, or indeed any preference at all? British governments, both Conservative and Labour, have rejected any suggestion that in normal circumstances domestic consumers should pay less than the world price for North Sea oil. The existence of a shortage does not offset the logic that underlies this non-discriminatory policy. Suppose for example that oil will fetch $100 a barrel on the international market. Then the value to the economy of a barrel of oil sold on that market is $100, since this is what domestic consumers in general would be willing to pay for the imports that it makes possible. If this amount is more than any one at home is willing to pay for the oil, then *prima facie* the balance of advantage lies in exporting it. In general, export prohibitions only serve to ensure that oil, gas, scrap metal, soya beans, or whatever the commodity may be is put to lower-value rather than higher-value use. Freedom to export should be the rule.

This argument still applies, moreover, to the case where there are limited domestic reserves of some non-renewable resource, as with gas from the UK Continental Shelf. A relevant consideration here is that the available reserves of a mineral are not a precisely known and immutable fact of geology. To establish their existence costs money, and like other economic activities it becomes more worth while at the margin if the prospective rewards are greater. In Britain, the oil companies rightly argue that freedom to export gas from the North Sea would increase the incentive to find new deposits of gas there. This however is not the fundamental point; and for all I know the British Gas

Corporation may be correct in its counter-argument that establishing the right to export would add little to prospective new discoveries of gas. The main point is that even in a situation where reserves were known and limited, the orthodox argument would still apply: if foreigners are willing to pay more at the margin, then exports represent a higher value use. The present and long-established restrictions on the export of gas from the United Kingdom are therefore not justified.

Contrary to what is often suggested, arguing in this way does not imply taking a myopic view, and sacrificing longer-term national gains to immediate profit. It may well be that oil and gas will be so much more valuable in the future, even allowing for the interest factor that has to be taken into account in such calculations, that governments should limit production now, and possibly also encourage imports, in order to conserve domestic resources for the future. This would be quite consistent with the orthodox economists' approach, because if the assumption is correct the effect of such conservation measures would be to substitute a future higher-value use for a present lower-value one. But it does not follow that overseas sales should be restricted, either now or at some future date. The case for giving more weight to the future, and less to the present, does not in any way establish a case for discriminating in favour of domestic consumers as against foreigners.

Let me add that, as in other applications of the willingness-to-pay criterion, freedom to export is a general presumptive rule, not a categorical imperative which admits of no exceptions. Restrictions on particular strategic exports may be justified on grounds of national defence. Taxes on commodity exports, which have the effect of reducing their flow, can in some circumstances be a useful instrument of policy in developing countries. Again, restrictions on food exports are justified in genuine national emergencies, as in some African countries at present, even though in themselves such restrictions will not give those in need the wherewithal to obtain food. All these, however, are exceptional or fringe cases in the modern world. They do not undermine the general orthodox argument that export restrictions based on essentialist ideas are contrary to the interests of a country that imposes them.

Security, international markets and reserve stocks

What about the second type of autarchic policy, that of minimizing dependence on imports? Here the orthodox view is more sympathetic, since it is obvious that serious consequences can result if a major international source of supply for key commodities like oil or gas is suddenly withdrawn or disrupted. But do-it-yourself economics, here as elsewhere, is no help. It leads people and governments both to exaggerate the risk and to use inappropriate ways of dealing with it.

On the first point, there is a chronic DIYE tendency to overstate the dangers of using overseas sources of supply. In part, this is because of the mistaken essentialist belief that there are national needs which have to be met. Another reason is that unreflecting centralism conjures up a picture in which imports are always bought directly from chronically unreliable foreign governments. More typically, however, it is not governments but business enterprises which ship the imports; and whether publicly or privately owned, these enterprises have an interest both in retaining profitable markets and in keeping their reputation for honouring contracts. Of course, and as recent history demonstrates, interruptions to imported supplies may none the less take place. But as British energy consumers need hardly be reminded after the recent coal strike, domestic supplies may also be subject to interruption and threats. Whether foreign sources are less reliable than domestic sources will depend on the circumstances. It cannot just be presumed.

On this question of security, orthodox economics has a strong positive message, which comes in two parts. In the first place, it points to the role of broad, well-functioning international markets as a means to reducing uncertainty and providing for emergencies. The existence of such markets, with free access to them on the part of buyers and sellers, provides the best assurance that purchases can always be made – an assurance which is reduced if countries resort to export prohibitions. The second part of the message is that in the case of storable commodities like oil, security can be improved, often at much lower cost than by substituting home production for imports, by the holding of ample reserve stocks. These stocks can be privately held, or they can be official, as in the case of the present US Strategic Petroleum Reserve: Mr MacQuedy has no prejudice against government action on these lines.

These two parts of the message are not distinct; for unless markets are allowed to function properly, the level of stocks will be lower than it should be. Holding stocks costs money. Why should any private agency go to the expense of keeping special emergency stocks, except perhaps for its own exclusive use, if it believes that in the event of a shortage the government will at once impose price controls to prevent so-called profiteering, and possibly also make supplies available from its own stocks at controlled prices? If stocks are to play their full potential role in providing insurance against emergencies, markets have to be allowed to set prices freely, and sales from government strategic stocks should be made by auction.

This orthodox message is a general one. But it is especially relevant in the energy field, because it is here in particular that risks are inevitable and the possible consequences of disturbance are still serious. Over the past decade or more, Western governments have taken action, individually and collectively, both to reduce dependence on imported oil and to provide for an emergency should it arise. In recent years, they have also made considerable progress in freeing internal markets for energy products. Where they have failed, largely I think because of the dominance of oversimplified economic notions, is in establishing and making acceptable the principle that even in times of perceived scarcity energy markets should be allowed to function freely and prices should reflect willingness to pay. Because of this failure, the risk of another energy crisis is greater than it need be, and the possible consequences more alarming. The contribution of markets to security is still not fully recognized.

Notes

1   Speech by Dr Garret FitzGerald at the Centre for European Policy Studies, Brussels, 22 November 1984.
2   *The Times*, 2 July 1981.
3   House of Commons, First Report from the Select Committee on Energy, Session 1980–81: *The Government's Statement on the New Nuclear Power Programme*, volume II: Minutes of Evidence (part 1), HC 114-II, London, HMSO, 1981, p. 39.
4   'How Switzerland has Benefited from the Market Approach', *Nuclear Engineering International*, July 1983.
5   L.R. Howles, 'Nuclear Station Achievement 1985', *Nuclear Engineering International*, August 1985.
6   First Report from the House of Commons Select Committee on Energy, 1980–81 (cited above), vol. II, part 1, p. 39.
7   *The Times*, 4 July 1985.
8   'Address to the Nation about Policies to Deal with the Energy Shortages', 7 November 1973.
9   Public Law 96–294, 30 June 1980, Section 100(a).
10 *The National Energy Program*, Department of Energy, Mines and Resources, Canada, Ottawa, 1980, p. 2.
11 Announcement in the House of Commons on depletion policy by the Secretary of State for Energy, Mr David Howell, 23 July 1980.
12 *Guardian*, spring 1979.
13 *The Observer*, 24 June 1979.
14 *Guardian*, 19 June 1979.
15 *Financial Times*, spring 1981.

4

ORTHODOX ECONOMISTS VERSUS THE PEOPLE

1095. (Viscount Falkland) Is it more basic than that? . . . Is this not a basic academic point which economists seem to have which is totally at odds with the view held by people in the practical business of creating wealth in this country which has to be resolved?

(Mr Withers) Yes, I think so.

(Chairman) Not all economists, to be fair. I think it is only some of them. (Minutes of Evidence taken before the House of Lords Select Committee on Overseas Trade, 26 March 1985)

The gulf between orthodox economic thinking and the intuitive notions of do-it-yourself economics is widest in the sphere of international economic relations in general, and trade policies in particular. The professionals, and those who think like them, are very much in a minority. Perhaps the sharpest difference between minority and majority lies in their respective conceptions of where national interests lie in international trade.

The art of breaking rules discreetly

Let me illustrate this first with reference to official policies towards exports. This is a subject on which DIYE is ambivalent. As I mentioned in my last lecture, it considers that for products which are labelled as essential, such as oil or gas in situations of perceived scarcity, exports should be prohibited however much foreigners are prepared to pay for them. But more typically, it takes the opposite view, that exports represent a benefit to the economy even if foreigners are only prepared to pay less than it costs to produce them. Essentialism fades into the background. Instead, the dominant idea is that of traditional mercantilism – the centuries-old belief that any reduction in imports or increase in exports will necessarily benefit the economy by improving the balance of payments and creating or safeguarding employment.

In consequence, DIYE thinking favours the use of export subsidies, both direct and indirect. But just as in the case of export restrictions on oil, various international agreements to which Britain is a party place limits on the extent to which such subsidies can be used. There are provisions of the Treaty of Rome which apply to members of the European Community; there are the relevant articles of the General Agreement on Tariffs and Trade (the GATT); and there is an OECD agreement which lays down guidelines for the use of official export credits.

Here again, therefore, a conflict of interest is seen as arising. The DIYE assessment is that the parties to the various agreements stand to gain if all of them observe the rules, but that each one would benefit from freedom to depart from the rules on its own. Hence each country's interest is thought to lie in using export subsidies to the fullest extent that it judges advantageous, short of breaking international agreements in a way that would give rise to countervailing or retaliatory actions by other governments. A similar precept holds good in relation to protective measures against imports, such as tariffs, quotas, and subsidies or preferences to domestic producers. The national interest is thought to lie in exploiting every protective device that comes to hand, subject again to the consequences that may flow from adverse reactions abroad.

In trade policy, the art of statesmanship is seen as being to sail as close to the wind as possible – to stretch or even evade internationally agreed rules, without actually breaking them. The guiding principle is that of opportunist mercantilism.

Let me offer some examples of current interventionist trade policies, both promotional and protectionist, which illustrate this principle in action. The examples are mostly British, but this is not because Britain stands out especially in these matters. British trade policies, which in any case are now largely the policies of the European Community, are broadly in line with those of most other industrial countries. It is true that British governments, regardless of party, have so far tended to take the protectionist side within the Community, while some observers consider that Community trade policies themselves are less liberal and more mercantilist than those of the United States, Japan and other OECD members. But these are differences only of degree.

Export subsidies

On the promotional side, the main form of direct and officially approved subsidies to exporters in Britain (as in other industrial countries) is the provision of official export financing at what are in effect subsidized rates. This applies mainly to capital goods exports and construction contracts, where terms of project financing may be just as important as price and quality of the bid in winning a contract. Exports are made available at fixed rates of interest which are generally below actual corresponding market rates, while the official premia that are charged for insurance against default on payments due for goods exported are below what the private market would charge. Further and substantial possibilities for subsidy can arise under so-called 'mixed credit' arrangements. Such arrangements chiefly apply to exports to developing countries that qualify for official aid from the exporting country. Part of the export deal is then financed from aid funds which are made available either in grant form or at low rates of interest, and which are tied to procurement in the donor country. In Britain such low-cost official financing is provided under the Aid and Trade Provision, established in 1977 by the then Labour government and enlarged by its successor. A recent case in point was the decision of British ministers in the spring of 1985 to extend to Thailand UK aid funding which would reduce the cost of a major package of equipment and supplies on offer to the Bangkok Mass Transit Authority.

In addition, direct subsidies to exports are also given by some authorities, in particular the US government and the European Commission, to make possible the sale abroad of agricultural products from embarrassingly large official stocks. In the case of the Commission, where disposals from the butter mountain are a long-standing example but sales of grain and sugar in particular have now assumed much greater importance, it is usual for the export subsidies to appear thinly disguised as 'restitution payments'.

Although direct subsidies are not necessarily involved, a further aspect of official export promotion should also be mentioned. This is the direct involvement of political leaders as salespersons and negotiators. In many countries including Britain, exporting is perceived as a contest among nations, in which ministers have to assume the role of general officers commanding, or at least of high-ranking special agents. Export contracts are turned into top-level political deals.

Official subsidies to exports may be indirect as well as direct. When a domestic subsidy is given to a firm or an industry or an activity, this will at the same time serve as a means of promoting exports and of giving protection against imports. In Britain, numerous official schemes have this dual effect: two examples are the special assistance that has been given in various ways to the shipbuilding industry, and the financial aid extended to tourist projects under section 4 of the Development of Tourism Act 1969.

Official suasion

Let me turn now to measures which are more directly and exclusively concerned with protection against imports. One aspect of current protectionism is that official pressure is brought to bear on businesses operating in the United Kingdom to limit imports and buy British. In the North Sea, for example, the Offshore Supplies Office, financed from public funds, is described as 'responsible to the Secretary of State [for Energy] for ensuring the maximum involvement of UK manufacturers, consultants, contractors and service companies in the provision of supplies and services to the offshore hydrocarbon industry'.[1] Officially, the government cannot lay down that preference should be given to British suppliers: this would be inconsistent with the Treaty of Rome, and indeed with other agreements. However, the Department of Energy is able to ensure that preferences are given none the less, since in deciding which applicants shall receive discretionary licences to operate in the North Sea the Secretary of State takes into account the companies' performance with respect to the local content of their purchases. Formal decency is preserved, since the relevant legislation refers only to 'providing full and fair opportunity to UK industry': no one can object to that. But in practice it is the fullness of the opportunity, rather than the fairness, that is stressed.

Other victims of official arm-twisting are the British subsidiaries of overseas vehicle firms. Both the Ford Motor Company of Britain and Vauxhall Motors have been pressed to raise not only the share of their British sales which comprises British-made cars but also the local content of the latter. In a Parliamentary reply this summer a minister in the Department of Trade and Industry expressed disappointment at the progress made by Vauxhall in these respects, and added:

> 'The Government looks to Vauxhall to provide a substantial and convincing demonstration of its willingness to move in the right direction and is continuing discussion aimed at achieving that objective.[2]

A related case is that of Nissan. The agreement which this company has signed with the Department of Trade and Industry, relating to its establishment of a manufacturing plant in Britain, includes provisions as to the local content of the company's purchases. Late in 1984 a senior official of the Department, Sir Anthony Rawlinson, was questioned before a House of Lords Select Committee on what such a clause in an agreement actually meant: did 'local' refer to the United Kingdom only, or to the Community as a whole? With what may have been injudicious candour, Sir Anthony replied that:

> It depends. We do not always put it in. In the case of Nissan, we meant in the United Kingdom.[3]

In the printed record, this response is accompanied by an explanatory footnote. Let me quote this pearl of Whitehall prose, as a demonstration of how to reposition a fig leaf that has slipped:

> The definition of local content encompasses components originating throughout the EEC, but it is the joint objective of the company and of the Department that the project should contribute to the development of long-term collaboration with local component and other supplying industries. There is every hope that, subject to the competitive capabilities of United Kingdom industry, a majority of the local content will in practice be British.

What this means is that the government will lean on Nissan, in the same way that it leans on Ford and Vauxhall, to buy British – without too much regard for what is in the Treaty of Rome.

Departmental protectionism

Besides influencing the conduct of private businesses, the present British government has likewise followed the example of its predecessors in operating its own direct protectionist policies. Examples are the close control exercised by the Department of Energy over coal imports, and – as it would now appear – of proposed imports of cheap electricity from France. But the most important aspect of direct public sector protectionism is procurement policy, and the long-established convention that national-ized industries and government departments should so far as possible buy British. It is almost invidious to take one example and not another; but the flavour is admirably conveyed in a news item which appeared a few years ago, and which casts a revealing light on the present govern-ment's often-expressed concern with getting value for money in public expenditure:

> The Government has assured the clothing industry that it will continue to press its 'Buy British' policy in its purchasing programme. The British Clothing Industry Association sought this official response because it feared some public authorities were buying the cheapest goods in the market.[4]

MFA and other VERs

In Britain as elsewhere, a now widely prevalent form of protectionism is that of discriminatory import restrictions.

Among the most prominent are the import quotas embodied in the Multi-Fibre Arrangement (MFA). The MFA dates from 1974, when it replaced the Long-Term Cotton Textiles Agreement of 1962. It is an elaborate and detailed set of provisions for regulating the course of international trade in textiles and clothing. Under its umbrella, Britain alone is at present a party to some 500 bilateral quota agreements with 27 exporting countries. A recent addition to the list provides an example of what is involved: there is a new quota on 'Men's and boys' shirts, of cotton, man-made textile fibres, of wool or of fine animal hair'[5] exported from Bangladesh. The agreement was made between the European Commission, acting on behalf of the United Kingdom, and the government of Bangladesh. The quota for this year was set at 2,200,000 shirts, with a slightly higher figure for 1986.

The exporting countries which have quotas within MFA are either developing countries, including India, Hong Kong and South Korea, or east European socialist countries. On the importing side are most of the Western industrial countries, including the European Community, the United States and Canada. It is worth noting that Japan, which is often portrayed as strikingly illiberal and restrictive in its treatment of imports, has imposed no MFA quotas on imports of textiles and clothing manufactures.

Now the articles of the GATT lay down as a general principle that trade among its members shall conform to the principle of non-discrimination, so that each member country is bound to extend equal treatment to all others. They further contain a general prohibition of import quotas; and Article XIX, which permits the use of tariffs or import quotas when imports 'cause or threaten to cause serious injury to competing domestic producers', also stipulates that such restrictions shall be non-discriminatory. How then is it possible for the highly discriminatory quotas of the MFA to be applied? The answer is that formally the restrictions are not applied by the importing countries. Rather than openly breaking the GATT rules, countries such as Britain have made agreements with the governments of particular exporting countries, by which those countries themselves accept the responsibility for restricting exports. The MFA is in fact negotiated and supervised within the GATT: it has been described as 'an internationally agreed derogation' from the GATT rules.

This same principle, of discriminatory import restrictions imposed, maintained and in part enforced from the exporting end, is now widely applied through what are known as Voluntary Export Restraint Agreements (VERs). Some of these are official, on a government to government basis, like the 1983 agreement between the European Commission and the government of Japan which provided for precise quantitative limits on Japanese exports of video cassette recorders to the European Community. Others are unofficial, made on an industry to industry basis, though few if any of these unofficial agreements could be made without government approval. The main importing countries concerned are the Community, the US and Canada. Most VERs apply to manufactured products. The exporting country chiefly affected is Japan, where various agreements limit the export of cars, light commercial vehicles, fork-lift trucks, TV sets and parts, hi-fi equipment, quartz watches, and I dare say other products – in addition to video cassette recorders. Other VERs have been negotiated with eastern European countries and some developing country manufacturing exporters, in particular Brazil, Taiwan and Thailand. The products mainly involved are footwear, TV sets and parts, radios, cutlery and ceramics. In addition, means have been found to restrict textiles and clothing imports from developing countries which are not parties to the MFA: much time for example has been spent in negotiations between officials of the European Commission and the government of Turkey over the precise number of T-shirts to be admitted into the

Community. In the case of steel, the Community itself has reluctantly agreed, after long and difficult negotiations, to place voluntary limits on the exports of certain products to the United States.

In the case of agricultural products, VERs are not usually thought necessary, since more direct restrictive measures, such as formal import quotas or the system of variable import levies operated by the Community, can be used instead. But a few years ago the European Commission negotiated with the governments of Brazil, Indonesia and Thailand VERs on their exports of manioc to the Community, on which an import levy could not be placed.

Why do the various exporting countries, whether in MFA or in these other VERs, agree to accept and operate quotas? One consideration is that the alternative may look worse. When it went along with the quotas on steel exports to the US, the European Commission was reported as being:

> ... forced to choose between agreeing an acceptable package or facing a complete ban on any further exports and imposing retaliatory trade restrictions on the US.[6]

A further point is that firms in the exporting countries do well out of the quota arrangements. If for example, and this is the present situation, exports of Japanese cars to Britain are restricted to 11 per cent of the market, then these cars can be sold here at a higher price than if there were no restriction. Who gets the benefit of the price difference will depend on how imports are restricted. Since in this instance as in other VERs the restrictions are imposed in the exporting country, rather than being operated by the British government through a tariff or a quota of its own, the gains from the higher prices accrue mainly to the Japanese firms involved. The effect is broadly the same as if the British government had imposed a tariff on these vehicles, collected the revenue from the tariff, and then disbursed the greater part of the proceeds through cheques made out to Toyota, Nissan and the other Japanese firms involved, with the rest going to their British counterparts. The present government has been greatly concerned about inflation – too much so, in the eyes of some of its critics. Yet it has followed the example of its predecessors, both Labour and Conservative, in embracing trade measures which artificially raise a wide range of product prices, and which cause a substantial part of the resulting gains to be made abroad rather than at home.

The prevalence of interventionism

The array of interventionist trade measures which I have described in barest outline is explained, in Britain as elsewhere, by a combination of influences on governments. Naturally, interest groups and lobbies are an ever-present and often powerful influence. Both jobs and profits are seen to be at stake, and well-orchestrated pressures are continuously brought to bear in all the areas of policy that I have mentioned. Almost always, these pressures are directed towards a greater degree of intervention in favour of domestic producers, whether through protection against imports or by promotion of exports. Except for consumers' organizations, and now and then businesses directly affected by restrictive trade measures, there are no lobbies for free trade. Even in prosperous times the interventionist pressures are strong and persistent. They are naturally intensified at times of high unemployment, so that those who lose jobs may find it difficult or impossible to get alternative work. Depression raises the stakes.

However, the activity of pressure groups is not the only factor involved: if it were, trade policies would now be, and would always have been, highly and unvaryingly interventionist. To influence events, the lobbies usually have to persuade others, who do not themselves stand to gain from what is proposed, that their cause has merit. In the famous passage which I quoted at the beginning of these lectures, Keynes considered whether it was vested interests or the ideas of economists which decided events. But in relation to trade policies, and I think in other areas too, both ideas and interests count, especially when they join forces. It is when pressure groups can draw support from widely accepted economic ideas, which as I have stressed need not be those of economists, that their campaigns are most likely to achieve results. This is the situation that prevails with respect to trade policies in many, perhaps most, countries today.

One reason for outside support of pleas for protection and subsidies is the feeling that this is only fair. This indeed is the official ground for many of the current British import restrictions, including those within the Multi-Fibre Arrangement: they are designed to prevent unacceptable 'social disruption'; and this is defined with reference to the economic losses which unregulated foreign competition would bring to workers and owners in specific industries. Overseas competition is seen as creating hard luck cases, and the government is seen as having a duty to help in such cases.

Orthodox economics recognizes this argument, but is concerned that too much weight should not be given to it. For one thing, the hard luck cases are not necessarily the poorest people, who may on the contrary suffer most from (for example) higher prices of electricity or of lower grade textile and clothing items. I doubt whether the shirts from Bangladesh, which Her Majesty's Government has been so concerned to restrict, would have been sold through Harrods. Again, it can be argued, as I already noted in my second lecture, that issues of poverty and need should be dealt with mainly through the social security system, and not by *ad hoc* handouts and concessions. Moreover, the argument for intervention on these grounds is logically an argument for slowing down all change in the interests of minorities who would be better off without it. Every one appreciates that the introduction of new products and processes helps to further economic progress, and no one seriously suggests that it should be stopped or restricted by law simply because it almost always harms the interests of some particular groups. But new possibilities for trade, which arise continually from the process of economic change at home and abroad, create exactly the same potential for progress. The fact is that there is no better reason for keeping out low-cost imports than there is for hindering the adoption of low-cost technologies.

The mercantilist rationale

Apart from considerations of fairness, interventionist trade measures, both protectionist and promotional, are largely justified within common sense economics, and in the eyes of governments and public opinion alike, by arguments about which I have so far said little. Soap operatics and unreflecting centralism have supporting parts, but the main role is played by other elements. One of these, naturally enough, is traditional mercantilism. Today's mercantilists, just like their predecessors, assume that specific jobs saved by import restrictions, or created by subsidized export deals, represent net additions to total employment. They rest their case on the kind of partial evidence that so impressed William McKinley, who from 1896 to 1900 was President of the United States, and of whom it has been said that:

> The great protected industries which he saw from his train window in travelling from Ohio to Washington assured him that he was right.[7]

For orthodox economics, however, this is only part of the story. Mr MacQuedy does not question the reality of the

view from today's train window, but he thinks that the
travellers are often wearing magnifying and rose-tinted
spectacles, and he is equally concerned with related
developments that are less noticeable. In his conception of
the economic system as a whole, the net effect on the
balance of trade and on the level of employment of
interventionist trade measures is slight and not necessarily
positive. If there is any net positive impact, it is both
limited and short term.

On this issue, orthodoxy and common sense are far
apart. Let me try to convey briefly, in a rather informal
way, why I believe Mr MacQuedy is right.

First, a general point. Keen mercantilists sometimes give
the impression that the measures they advocate somehow
hold the key to higher prosperity and employment. But as a
general proposition this does not bear examination. If we
take a historical or an international perspective, it is clear
that other and more fundamental forces must be at work.
Take for example the evidence of recent history. During the
1950s and 1960s rates of unemployment in the OECD
countries, including Britain, were remarkably low by
historical standards. For the ten-year period from 1960 to
1969 the average rate for the UK was not much over 1.5 per
cent. Over the four years from 1982 to 1985 the corresponding figure will be over 11 per cent, nor is this generally
expected to come down much in the near future. Whatever
the explanation for this depressing and largely unforeseen
change in national economic fortunes, it cannot be attributed to a falling off in official mercantilist zeal – even had
such a falling off occurred, which it has not. Still less could
such a hypothesis explain the general tendency to higher
unemployment in the Western world as a whole, since any
positive employment gains in one country that are due to
trade interventionism alone are made at the expense of
others.

A similar conclusion emerges from international com-
parisons at the present time. Current and prospective

unemployment rates in Western countries vary greatly: the mid-1985 OECD *Economic Outlook* points to the possibility of:

> . . . a further widening of European unemployment differentials in 1986, with rates ranging from 1¼ per cent in Switzerland to more than 21 per cent in Spain.[8]

No one would seriously suggest that these wide differences can be to any extent explained by differences in the degree of resort to *ad hoc* protection and promotion, with the more interventionist countries coming off better.

Hence trade interventionist measures cannot be thought of as a deciding influence on unemployment levels, nor is this what most serious mercantilists would claim. Their case is that for any one country such measures can act as a stimulus, while failure to make use of them in a world where other countries do so will necessarily be a drag on prosperity. By contrast, the orthodox position is that visible employment gains in favoured sectors of the economy, which benefit from subsidies or restrictions, are offset by consequential though less visible losses elsewhere.

In support of this latter view, let me list some ways in which trade interventionism favouring one sector of the economy can be damaging to others. First, import restrictions like voluntary export restraint agreements raise prices to domestic consumers, and this leaves them with less to spend on other products. Second, subsidies to exports and to particular industries have to be financed from taxation, which leaves taxpayers with less to spend; and taxpayers likewise suffer if government procurement policies give preferences to high-cost domestic producers. Third, restrictions on imports used by businesses, such as cotton yarn from Hong Kong or fork-lift trucks from Japan, raise costs to the firms concerned, and make it harder for them to compete; and the same result follows if governments

compel firms to increase the local content of their purchases. Fourth, if protected or subsidized firms can obtain
labour or finance more easily, their competitive position is
stronger in relation to other firms within the economy.
Fifth, if imports from particular countries are held down,
this in turn reacts on exports to those countries, and on
opportunities for exporters. Sixth and last, if and in so far as
strong and widespread trade interventionism is effective in
reducing expenditure on imports and raising export
receipts, this is likely to cause the exchange rate to be
higher than it otherwise would have been. For some or all of
these reasons, the relative importance of which will vary
from case to case in ways that can only be partly traced, the
sectors which are not favoured by restrictions and subsidies
will suffer. Any stimulus that these measures provide in
some areas of an economy will be offset by adverse effects
elsewhere. This argument would apply even if interventionist measures never provoked imitative or retaliatory action
on the part of other countries, which in fact they often do.
The main effect of *ad hoc* import restrictions, export
subsidies and subsidies of other kinds to domestic producers of traded goods is to weaken the position of the firms
and industries that can compete without these forms of
assistance. This is not a recipe for prosperity, nor indeed for
fairness.

The nationalist dimension

Nevertheless, most governments seem unimpressed by
these arguments, partly perhaps because ministers and
their advisers are not always well acquainted with them.
Another reason is that traditional mercantilism is often
reinforced, not only by considerations of fairness, but also
by economic nationalism. This combination of ideas is not
new. Here is a revealing summary which I came across of

the economic thinking of the Spanish military dictator General Primo de Rivera in the 1920s:

> Haunted by dreams of autarky, he was pained by the French wines and American cars of the upper classes and the preference Spanish doctors showed for imported scalpels. Every article that could be produced or grown in Spain must be produced, regardless of production costs: hence 'intervention' to save domestic coal production, lead, and resin; hence the attempt to create a national car industry, to finance home-grown cotton by a levy on imported cotton, to intensify 'cerealist' [grain] policies. Thus the Spanish economy fell into the hands of committees regulating everything from hydroelectric power to the rabbit-skin industry.[9]

Much the same could have been said about General Franco's economic policies, until the liberalization of the Spanish economy began in the late 1950s. As to attitudes and broad policies, as distinct from political régime, there is not so much to choose between Spain of the 1920s and India over the past four decades. These are not exceptional cases. All over the world, trade intervention has been used, and continues to be used, as a means of promoting specific developments, and asserting national identity, without much regard to market opportunities or costs. Self-reliance, like self-sufficiency, is seen as a magic formula for success.

Much the same nationalist attitudes, slightly watered down, can be found today in Britain and some other industrial countries. In particular, official support for 'high-tech' projects and programmes has been influenced by the state of mind that I have termed bipartisan technological chauvinism. The development of home-grown technology, with public funding and protection against ideas and equipment from abroad, is seen as conferring on a country independence, prestige and balance of payments gains. Mercantilism joins with patriotic sentiment, and with soap operatic visions of authentically native 'sunrise industries'. The programmes which are born of these ideas soon gain further support and momentum because of the powerful vested interests they create.

Nationalist arguments do not impress Mr MacQuedy. Protecting or subsidizing supposedly advanced indigenous developments makes no net contribution to employment, and does nothing to reduce poverty or inequality. In these respects, it is no different from less glamorous forms of trade interventionism, like keeping out low-cost coal or sugar. As for arguments of strategy, self-reliance and prestige, these are not only exaggerated by interested parties but also open to question. A country does not gain in defensive capability, nor does it increase its freedom of action, by saddling its business firms and armed services with uncompetitive high-cost systems.

Autonomy and trade unilateralism

The orthodox economic view, then, is that discriminatory trade interventions are generally contrary to the interests of the countries that make use of them. There are exceptions to this, such as the case of moderate temporary protection for infant industries, and these are systematically spelled out in the professional literature; but I doubt whether any of the measures that I described in the first part of this lecture can count as such an exception. Thus countries like Britain would be better off if they adopted liberal trade policies. Moreover, this holds true for any one country, or for a group of countries like the European Community, regardless of whether the example is followed by others.

This last conclusion is not a popular one. Most people will tell you that the right to protect and subsidize, if necessary by means that are contrary to the spirit if not the letter of international agreements, is one that every state must exercise in a world where it is exercised by others. In Britain today, and I believe in other countries too, the government is widely criticized for playing the game of international trade according to rules which other governments feel free to break. Do-it-yourself economics holds that unilateral free trade is open to the same objections as unilateral disarmament.

The orthodox viewpoint makes two concessions, of expediency only, to this point of view. There may be a case now and then for using interventionist measures for purely tactical reasons, as a bargaining counter. More important, it is politically easier for governments to make what are widely seen as concessions on the trade front if other countries are joining them as part of a wider international bargain. Reciprocal concessions on tariffs and quotas have in fact made a large contribution to freeing international trade in the period since the Second World War. But though reciprocity may be tactically convenient or even necessary as a basis for trade negotiations, it has no deeper justification. The fundamental point is that traditional mercantilist ideas are mistaken. Even from a strictly national viewpoint, therefore, the so-called concessions that are made in giving up interventionist trade policies actually represent on balance gains rather than losses. Nor is the right to protect and subsidize at will a basic attribute of national sovereignty. The freedom for governments to act against the national interest is hardly a great prize, and their real autonomy is not reduced by giving up the right to bestow *ad hoc* favours on every influential pressure group.

From the orthodox standpoint, current trends in Western trade policies are disturbing. In particular, it is a sad reflection on present-day economic statesmanship in countries such as Britain that it views the extensive and growing network of discriminatory export restraint agreements as a positive achievement. In this respect as in some others, official policies rest on a conception of national interests which is pre-economic.

Notes

1   Memorandum of understanding between Department of Energy and United Kingdom Offshore Operators Association Limited, 3 November 1975.
2   *Financial Times*, 8 August 1985.
3   Minutes of Evidence taken before the House of Lords Select Committee on Overseas Trade, 20 November 1984.
4   *Financial Times*, late 1981.
5   This is the official description of MFA category number 8.
6   *Financial Times* report 1984.
7   H. Wayne Morgan, *William McKinley and his America*, Syracuse University Press, 1963, p. 60.
8   OECD, *Economic Outlook* 37, June 1985, p. 29.
9   Raymond Carr, *Spain 1808–1975*, Oxford, Clarendon Press, 1982.

5

DIYE PLUS THE LOBBIES: COUNTING THE COST

It has not been recorded that the dramatic appeal made by a thousand leading economists to Mr Hoover in 1930, asking him to veto the Smoot-Hawley Bill, caused that gentleman to hesitate before approving the bill. (E.E. Schattschneider, Policies, Pressures and the Tariff, *Englewood Cliffs, New Jersey, Prentice-Hall, 1935, p. vii)*

I have described some characteristic differences between economic orthodoxy and intuitive economics, and shown how these differences can affect actual policies. In this lecture I want to consider two questions that naturally arise. First, why is it that in some areas of economics, but not in others, ideas that are characteristically professional have so little influence? This leads on to a second and much larger issue: How much does this lack of influence matter?

The two tiers of economics revisited

I think the first of these questions is easy to answer in broad terms. I spoke in my first lecture about two tiers of economic problems and issues. One is that of macroeconomics. The second has provided the subject matter of my last three lectures. It is chiefly in this second tier that do-it-yourself economics holds sway.

Let me illustrate these points with reference to two issues of policy which are actively debated in Britain today. First, there is the question of whether or not the United Kingdom should participate in the managed exchange-rate arrangement of the European Monetary System (the EMS). Second, there is the problem of how best to give effect to the generally accepted idea that the government should control the rate of growth of the money supply. For example, which of the various measures of the stock of money is the right one to take? Should British monetary policy focus on M0, M1, M2, M3 or PSL2, or should it take into account changes in more than one of these, and possibly in other indicators also?

These are live issues and important ones. In deciding them, ministers may be influenced by political as well as more technical considerations: the question of joining the EMS, for instance, has a political aspect to which some people would attach a good deal of weight. But the issues *are* plainly technical, and how they are decided is unlikely to make a big difference to the relative position of particular sectional groups. Hence the debate is largely restricted to specialists of various kinds; and there are no lobbies, demonstrations, publicity campaigns or constituency pressures. In such a context, it is reasonable to think of governments and their advisers as guardians of the public interest, trying to find the best way of dealing with issues that bear on the general welfare of the nation as a whole.

It is worth noting that throughout his career, both as an academic and an official, these were the kinds of issues that Keynes himself was largely concerned with.[1] His first book, published in 1913, was on Indian currency and finance. It arose from his experience in the job that he took after graduating from Cambridge, as an administrative civil servant in what was then the India Office. In it he discussed questions, such as whether or not the India of the Raj should have its own central bank, which though important were of interest to, and decided by, a restricted group of influential people. There was no lobbying or agitation on these subjects, either in India or in Britain, no powerful interests to be outmanoeuvred or bought off. The governments concerned could make a detached assessment, and were genuinely searching for the best set of arrangements that could be made. In weighing alternatives, no profound knowledge of Indian history or society was required, nor did Keynes ever visit India. Policy could be influenced, had to be influenced, by impartial expert advice: hence the importance of ensuring that the right kind of high-level expertise was brought to bear within government. Even in the much broader questions which later engaged Keynes's attention – the return to the gold standard in 1925, the handling of the economic crisis and depression of the 1930s, the problems of war finance in Britain, the negotiation of the wartime financial agreements which established the International Monetary Fund, the World Bank, and the post-war international monetary régime – it was possible to take much the same view of the role of governments, and of economists as their chief mentors.

Admittedly, not all macroeconomic issues are of this rather antiseptic kind, with a high perceived technical content and a relatively low political one. Sometimes interest groups are very much involved. Consider, for example, the argument that the present British government should adopt a less austere fiscal policy stance, and permit a rather higher public sector borrowing requirement. Since if they did so this might well lead to higher levels of public expenditure, including capital expenditure on roads, housing and so on, it is not hard to predict which side the construction industry favours in the debate over fiscal policy. Other instances of the same kind can readily be found. All the same, I think it is a valid generalization that national rather than sectional aspects are those mainly taken into account when macroeconomic issues are under review. Of course, governments may try to buy votes at a national level, as well as by dispensing favours to particular groups. Most people now take it for granted that a British government's last budget before a general election will offer more concessions than if it had come earlier or later, under otherwise similar conditions. But the scope for this is limited, and it remains true that fiscal and monetary policies are influenced by considerations where expertise is sought.

Again, largely because of their more obviously technical character, macroeconomic issues provide less suitable material for widely held intuitive convictions. It is true that the subject of money has held an irresistible attraction for amateur theorists down the ages. But this is not an exception to my rule, since most of the time these amateurs have been few in number, and neither representative nor influential. Theirs is not the economics of Everyman.

There is, however, one major exception, where do-it-yourself economics invades the domain of macroeconomic policy. This concerns the problem of unemployment. In viewing this problem and possible ways of dealing with it, DIYE makes the unspoken assumption that the level of output in the economy is to be taken as given. Hence it is believed that the introduction of any labour-saving change will increase unemployment: technical progress is seen as necessarily reducing the number of jobs available. Similarly, it is thought that administrative measures to reduce the size of the labour force – such as compulsory reductions in working hours, enforced early retirement or restrictions on immigration – will necessarily ease the unemployment problem. The fact that conventional economic analysis does not lend support to these propositions has not greatly weakened their hold on public opinion, and sometimes also on ministers and officials.

All the same, and despite the qualifications that I have just made, I think it is broadly true that in relation to macroeconomic questions, my first tier of economics, Keynes was right: here the ideas of economists do generally count for more than vested interests. But in my second tier, as I have shown, what governments chiefly respond to are the mutually reinforcing influences of the lobbies and of ways of thinking that are pre-economic. Economists' ideas, where they are noticed at all, are often set aside.

Why economists fail to influence people

Why is it that long-established economic orthodoxy has made so little impact on the ways of thinking of informed, intelligent and disinterested lay persons? Certainly the main reason is that the ideas of DIYE have a strong intuitive appeal, so strong that it may not even cross the minds of those who hold them that any alternative could exist. But part of the explanation lies with us, the professionals. To an extent which is quite striking, even disturbing, we have failed to impress others with our point of view.

One reason for this is that not all economists share that point of view. Some are highly critical of the orthodox principles of individualism, reliance on markets and prices, decentralization and non-discrimination including free trade. I shall have something to say about these dissenters in my final lecture. But those professionals who would actually side with do-it-yourself economics against orthodoxy are a minority. Most of us, on the left of the conventional political spectrum as well as the right, are conditioned by our training to view what I have called second tier questions through orthodox spectacles. In fact, I would say that economists are at present more agreed – perhaps I should say less disunited – on these questions, where they are typically not listened to, than on the macroeconomic issues where they often are. But this consensus in favour of orthodox as opposed to intuitive ways of thinking has not led to a general acceptance of them outside the profession.

In part, this may be due to the conspicuous disagree-

ments in macroeconomics and elsewhere, which make for
public scepticism about what any of us may have to say on
any subject. But there are other reasons too. One concerns
those economists of orthodox leanings who think that
second-tier issues matter. Here I feel there is a major
problem of communication. With honourable exceptions,
starting with David Hume and Adam Smith and continuing to Samuel Brittan and Milton Friedman in our own
day, we have failed to argue our case persuasively, in
language that can be understood by educated non-
specialists. The growing professionalization of economics,
while natural and in general to be welcomed, has worsened
this problem in recent decades. Economists have become
increasingly preoccupied with each other's thoughts and
writings, and less interested in what any one else might
think. This happens with every profession, but it is more
unfortunate for us than for others.

A further reason is that much of the professional support
for the orthodox point of view is sporadic, lukewarm or
reluctant, because interest and attention are directed
elsewhere. For the past half-century, and despite a reaction
during the past 15 years or so, economics has been
dominated by a view of the subject and of the world as a
whole which I call *macro-supremacist*. On this view, the
important problems, both intellectual and practical, lie in
the domain of macroeconomics, while other issues are by
comparison of small account. This concentration on
macroeconomics has had two natural results. The extent to
which other economic policies are dominated by intuition,
rather than more distinctively professional ideas, has often
gone unobserved; and when observed, it has not necessarily
been seen as a matter for much concern.

The rise of macro-supremacist views

This brings me to the second and larger of my two
questions: How much does it matter if do-it-yourself

economics prevails, at any rate within my second tier? In approaching this question, I would like for a moment to put on one side the main theme of these lectures. I want to turn from the foreground of my picture to the background, to set my argument in a wider context of economic ideas and events.

Let me start with a well-worn but helpful metaphor. Economic policy within each country is concerned with the size of the cake and the way in which it is divided up – that is, with production and distribution or, in current textbook language, efficiency and equity. Economic efficiency in this sense is conventionally thought of as having three aspects. One of these is the concern of macroeconomics as I have defined it. From this point of view, efficiency means making full use of the resources that are available to an economy at a given time – in particular, resources of labour – so that the *productive potential* of the economy is realized. In a developed country such as Britain, the best single indicator of success in this respect is the unemployment rate – or, more strictly, the difference between the current and prospective unemployment rate and whatever is thought to be the minimum sustainable rate.

As the years pass, however, the productive resources available within an economy will normally increase: the labour force grows; the capital stock is built up; knowledge and skills accumulate; and technical progress occurs, so that labour and other inputs can be used more productively. This is the second aspect of efficiency – the *growth* of productive potential over time, and in particular, the growth of productivity.

The third aspect is what economists call *resource allocation* – in other words, making the best use of the resources available to an economy within any given period. This is in fact my second tier of economic issues. The issues largely concern what goods and services are produced, and how they are produced; and underlying the characteristic economists' approach to this is a perception of the way in which free markets, with prices responding to changes in demand and supply, can help to achieve a more efficient outcome.

Now when the Great Depression of the 1930s swept over the world, it swept over the orthodox economic establishment as well. The professionals had not foreseen this calamity; they were unable to explain it convincingly; and they had no agreed remedy to offer which carried conviction. The long-established professional view of the economy as a self-equilibrating system, in which involuntary unemployment was not a serious problem, was undermined by events. Since it was through changes in relative prices that the self-equilibrating forces were supposed to act, belief in the efficacy of prices and markets was likewise undermined.

In this situation, the Keynesian system offered both a diagnosis and a prescription. At the analytical level, it gave reasons for believing that modern capitalist economies had a chronic tendency towards deficiency of demand, which explained why unemployment had become a persistent and serious problem. The remedy lay in government action, largely through fiscal and monetary policies, to maintain demand at a sufficiently high – though not excessive – level. Hence as I noted in my first lecture, the central task of economic policy was now viewed as being the management of demand.

From this Keynesian standpoint, it was the first aspect of economic efficiency, full employment, that counted. By comparison, the third aspect, the allocation of resources, was unimportant. In dealing with it, prices and markets could broadly be relied on, but only because the issues involved were minor. I should add that Keynes himself, and many of his professional associates and followers also, were neither socialists nor believers in detailed central planning. The fact remains that one of the results of the Keynesian revolution, and a long-lasting one, was to play down the significance of resource allocation issues, and to stress the limitations rather than the uses of markets.

As to the second aspect of economic efficiency, the growth of productive potential over time, the view became widely accepted in the 1950s and 1960s that full employment was in itself a strongly positive factor, through its effects on investment and attitudes to change. Hence if the first aspect of economic efficiency was taken care of, this would help substantially with the second – and indeed with the third as well, since full employment would also over time weaken sectional and mercantilist pressures. Successful demand management was thus seen as the key to improving economic efficiency in all its aspects. Questions of income distribution apart, economic policy was macroeconomics with trimmings.

Macroeconomic policies: the continuing debate

In most of the OECD countries, this view of the world continued to gain ground up to at any rate the end of the 1960s. The post-Keynesian consensus became widely established as the new orthodoxy, at least in relation to macroeconomics which was what chiefly counted. Then, like the old orthodoxy in the Great Depression of the 1930s, it was shaken by a combination of unforeseen events and professional criticism. A new series of major debates was initiated within the profession, more prolonged and less one-sided than those of the 1930s, though once again they were mainly centred on macroeconomic issues.

The events that undermined the new orthodoxy can largely be summed up in a single ugly but convenient word, *stagflation*, that is, the state of affairs in which high rates both of unemployment and of inflation persist together. Accepted demand management policies could not prevent the onset of stagflation in the mid-1970s, nor did they offer an effective formula for coping with it once it had become established. Both as an intellectual system and as a guide to action the post-Keynesian consensus was challenged by the rival monetarist approach, within which the likelihood of accelerating inflation, even in the presence of higher unemployment rates, had been foreseen and explained. As events unfolded in the 1970s, the debate was extended from the groves of academe to the corridors of power.

The issue is often described as one of Keynesianism versus monetarism, but it goes wider than that. It also goes deeper than the practical question of the importance of monetary policy as such. When Denis Healey as Chancellor of the Exchequer accepted in 1976 the principle of monetary targets in the United Kingdom, he was not I think committing himself to the doctrines laid down at about the same time in Milton Friedman's Nobel memorial lecture. He was responding to the needs of the situation as he (and I imagine his officials) saw them. On the other hand, the Prime Minister of the day, James Callaghan, did rather surprisingly identify himself with underlying monetarist doctrine when he said in his speech to the Labour Party Conference of September 1976:

> We used to think that you could just spend your way out of recession, and increase employment, by cutting taxes and boosting government spending. I tell you in all candour that this option no longer exists, and that in so far as it ever did exist, it worked by injecting inflation into the economy.[2]

No doubt the present Conservative Chancellor, Nigel Lawson, would be happy to endorse this statement today.

The main issue in the debate is not the choice of particular instruments or measures, but the properties and behaviour of economic systems. Although the labels are not ideal, the two rival schools of thought can be described as post-Keynesian and 'new classical'. Like Keynes himself, the post-Keynesians view modern market economies as subject to disturbances which automatic mechanisms will not smooth out, so that there is no presumption that output will stay close to the level corresponding to the lowest sustainable rate of unemployment. They also believe – though often with more reservations and qualifying clauses than 15 years ago – that financial policies, possibly supported by incomes policies, can do much to correct this deficiency. Their view of the world can thus be summarized as stability pessimism combined with policy optimism. The new classical position is the reverse of this. Its adherents share with Keynes's opponents of the 1930s the belief that there are strong self-equilibrating forces at work in market economies. They are stability optimists. At the same time, they stress the limitations – some of them would say, the impotence – of official stabilization policies.

One result of the debate, and of the chastening experiences of Western economies in recent years, has been to weaken the hold of macro-supremacist ideas. This can be seen both in professional writings and in the actions of governments. Many of the post-Keynesians now accept that demand management policies will work better if the functioning of markets, and particularly of labour markets, is improved. This establishes a link with their opponents, who are strongly market-oriented. In spite of the wide differences, there is a shared interest in the interactions between the behaviour of individual markets and that of the system as a whole; and there is often agreement on specific measures to improve resource allocation – or, as they are often now termed, 'supply side' measures. There is also an uneasy consensus which embraces most post-Keynesians and monetarists – to which, however other 'new classical' economists are not parties – that economic policy should be viewed in terms of both demand side and supply side measures, which are to be seen as complementary and mutually supporting.

The current economic strategy

This middle-of-the road consensus is reflected in the broad

economic strategy that has now been adopted in virtually all the OECD countries. There is a common concern with inflation, and a common emphasis on maintaining firm control over the money supply, limiting both public expenditure and fiscal deficits, and reducing the scope of government regulations and controls. As compared with ten to fifteen years ago, demand management is no longer the jewel in the crown of economic policy, and official thinking has moved in a market-oriented direction.

So far, however, – and here I return to my main theme – this change of direction has not greatly affected my second tier of economic issues. The main impetus for change has come from the pressure of events and the ferment of ideas in the world of macroeconomics; and the chief official agencies favouring change have been ministries of finance and central banks, which are preoccupied with the ever-pressing first-tier problems of inflation, public finance, money supply and exchange rates. While it is true that reigning economic doctrines are no longer macro-supremacist, the debate on ideas and policy, as well as the day-to-day thinking of governments, is still macrocentric – and understandably so. Second tier issues, though now seen as more pertinent than before, still remain subsidiary. The supremacy of do-it-yourself economics has not yet been threatened, and the informal alliance between DIYE and the lobbies retains its power to influence events and measures. The clearest evidence of this is to be found in trade policies, where interventionism by Western governments has actually become more widespread and accepted in recent years.

How much does this matter? Despite the shift in opinion that I have just described, I believe that many of my professional colleagues would respond to this question with a dismissive shrug of the shoulders. A common professional criticism of these lectures will be that Henderson spent his time discussing small questions on which 90 per cent of literate economists have been agreed for 200 years, instead of addressing the issues that really matter. Let me explain why my own perspective is different.

I referred just above to three aspects of efficiency in the economic sense: full employment, economic growth and improved resource allocation. I showed how it was natural from the standpoint of Keynesian ideas to think of the first of these as not only the most important in itself, but also the key to the other two. Let me now offer some reasons for believing that on the contrary it is in the third area of policy, the allocation of resources, that the key is to be found.

Misdirected investment

Some years ago I gave a series of radio talks which I called, with due acknowledgement to Oscar Wilde, 'The Unimportance of Being Right'. My subject was two large British public sector programmes, the Concorde aircraft and the Second UK Nuclear Power Programme. I described these as two of the three worst civil investment decisions in the history of mankind, the third being the Soviet counterpart to Concorde. Events since I gave these talks have not led me to revise my judgement on the costs associated with these two programmes. If however I were now to undertake further research on this broad theme, I think I would direct my attention to some major ventures in other countries, including the long-established nuclear power programme in India.

I mention these expenditure programmes because they have been conspicuously costly, but also in order to emphasize two points. First, they involve the allocation of resources. It is necessary to make this statement of the obvious, since a surprising number of economists have the mistaken idea that resource allocation is only a matter of what happens to relative prices in an otherwise unchanging world. On the contrary, it extends to the choice of investments. Second, let me stress that it is no accident that my examples are in the public sector. Of course, private firms can make expensive mistakes; but the fact that they are dependent on markets sets a limit to the amounts they can lose. In the public sector the limits are less well drawn, and often ineffective. Major programmes which yield few outputs, or even none at all, can acquire a status and momentum which are almost unassailable. The fast reactor programme in Britain is an example. If it had never been embarked on, more than 30 years ago now, little would have been lost; if it were abandoned now, I believe that the same would hold true. The whole nuclear power programme in India rests on an intuitive technocratic vision of the early 1950s, well laced with a brand of do-it-yourself economics which eminent scientists find congenial. The results in terms of costs incurred and actual kilowatt-hours generated have been consistently disappointing; but so powerful is the vision that it is proof against all evidence and experience.

Industrial strategies

The same imperviousness to evidence can be seen in the industrial policies pursued over the past four decades by successive British governments. I believe that the long and continuing sequence of assisted programmes, subsidized ventures, officially arranged mergers, support for lame ducks and selective aid for special cases has had, and will continue to have, adverse effects on British economic performance. Obvious fiascos, of which the De Lorean, Lear Fan and Nexos projects are recent examples, are only a part of the story. In so far as these were due to straight commercial misjudgement, I find them less depressing than schemes which owed their support to the combination of DIYE, nationalist sentiment and the natural desire of ministers and officials to play, and be seen to be playing, an active role. It is this combination which ensures that past failures, where they are noticed at all, do not undermine the widespread and continuing support in Britain for an activist industrial strategy.

Let me add that Britain is not at all an exception in this respect. It would be easy to compile a list of cautionary examples from the industrial policies of other countries – large and small, rich and poor. Nor is it only national governments that are involved. I believe that some of the much-applauded programmes of the European Commission in the field of advanced technology will worsen the problem they are designed to cure. All over the world, ambitious notions of industrial strategy provide the impetus for misdirected investments.

Investment and growth

So far I have spoken of particular investment or expenditure programmes. But resource allocation goes wider than this. It extends, for example, to the division of investment between the public and the private sector. Again, at the level of the economy as a whole, the question arises as to how the total resources available will be divided between, on the one hand, investing for the future – through expenditure on equipment and buildings, research and development, and education and training – and on the other hand, current consumption. This key ratio of total investment to national product is itself one of the topics that comes under the heading of the allocation of resources.

From this a striking conclusion can be drawn. My second aspect of economic efficiency is the growth of productive potential over time. But this will be strongly influenced by the total rate of investment and by the return on the particular projects which make up the total: growth, in other words, depends in large part on the quantity and quality of future-directed expenditure. To the extent that this is so, the second aspect of economic efficiency has no independent status, but merges into the third. Economic growth itself becomes a matter of resource allocation.

Growth performance and trade régimes

Viewed in this way, the issue of growth is linked to that of the role of markets. The possibly close connection between a country's growth performance and the extent of its reliance on markets was brought home to me in the late 1960s by a combination of personal experience and some notable work by other economists. Both the experience and the books and articles I read related to developing countries and their choice of trade policies. Up to then it had been generally assumed, by economists and practical men alike, that in these countries there was little scope for relying on prices and markets, certainly less than in the industrial countries where post-Keynesian orthodoxy in any case played down their role. As part of this view, it was thought that the developing countries would be wise to reduce their dependence on trade and world markets, and to operate highly regulated trade and payments systems. Events and professional argument have now discredited this notion. It is now widely agreed that those developing countries that established open trade régimes, which were relatively free from administrative controls and did not discriminate against exports, were able thereby to achieve higher sustained rates of growth in output and standards of living. The outstanding successes in this respect have been Hong Kong, South Korea, Singapore and Taiwan. Their achievements have matched those of Japan.

At the other end of the spectrum is Ghana. It presents the rare case of a country which has actually become poorer compared with a quarter of a century ago, when it was the most prosperous state in black Africa. The main single element in Ghanaian prosperity was the flourishing cocoa industry which had been built up by peasant proprietors. A recent study describes it as having been 'garrotted' by government policies.[3] Chiefly, these policies comprised low controlled prices to producers, taxes on cocoa exports, and a persistently and grossly overvalued exchange rate. For those who believe that what happens to relative prices within an economy is a matter of minor importance, the case of Ghanaian cocoa, as indeed the whole depressing sequence of events there, is worth pondering.

Let me underline that all the cases that I have cited, in developed and developing countries alike, involve different facets of resource allocation which are inseparable in the real world: prices, markets, investment and international trade. I began by discussing a range of misconceived investment projects. But in all of these governments had deliberately set aside market criteria, and in effect imposed their own prices – either explicitly through subsidies, or implicitly through hidden preferences and administrative regulations. In so doing, they turned their backs on the opportunities offered, both for buying and for selling, by international markets – just as governments have also done in creating administered trade régimes, as in the Multi-Fibre Arrangement or the Community's Common Agricultural Policy. In some cases, they also turned their backs on ideas because they were foreign. At the level of particular sectors and investment projects, this has brought low returns or actual losses. Pursued on an economy-wide scale, as in many developing countries, it has been the chief retarding influence on economic growth.

The distortion of incentives

A related and fundamental point is this. In every country, the use by governments of discretionary instruments of economic policy is liable to have damaging effects on growth, because of the way in which these distort incentives. Put simply, growth arises from innovation and change within society; and individuals and enterprises make innovations, and initiate or accept changes, because it is in their interests to do so. They are motivated by both the expectation of gain and the fear of loss. But typically, when governments make *ad hoc* use of licences, prohibitions, import levies or quotas, subsidies, procurement preferences or even informal arm-twisting, the effect is to reward one particular group within a country at the expense of every one else. This, of course, is why the interest groups are so active and well organized. The more these administrative devices are used, the more the fortunes of firms and industries, of employees and owners, depend on their success, not in providing what people are willing to pay for, but in persuading those in authority to adopt measures which are contrary to the interests of the rest of the community and which retard the process of change. In so far as political processes take over the functions of competitive markets, it is no longer enterprise or efficiency that brings rewards, but successful lobbying, backed by expertise in the ways and personalities of government and in the arcane complexities of official regulations. Historically it is the great achievement of the market economy to have made sustained economic growth possible, by establishing a sphere of activity in which the self-interest of individuals, together with their skills and creative energies, are harnessed to socially beneficial ends. Modern governments, under the influence of pressures and naive economic perceptions, are often ready to cast this advantage aside.

Lastly, let me recall a point I made earlier in this lecture. Many post-Keynesian economists would broadly agree with their new classical opponents that if markets are able to operate more freely this is likely to assist in bringing down the current high unemployment rates in many OECD countries. It may also help in the longer term to reduce the minimum sustainable rate of unemployment in some of these economies. If this is true, then the first aspect of economic efficiency, as well as the second, falls partly at least under the heading of resource allocation.

In the last half of this lecture I have been arguing a case. I have argued that the prosperity of countries depends in large part on how far their governments are prepared to allow choices, and especially investment choices, to be influenced by market forces in general and international market opportunities in particular. Let me emphasize that in putting this case I am not trying to remove macroeconomic issues from the stage: far from it. And though I have given reasons for questioning the macro-supremacist view which prevailed for so long after the Keynesian revolution, I can well see the attractions of that view. I have reached a different position myself through a combination of personal experience, events on the world scene, and professional arguments; but I do not rule out the possibility that some time in the future these combined influences, in a new and changing situation, might cause me to move in the reverse direction.

Meanwhile, however, I find it hard to sympathize with those economists who think that resource allocation is synonymous with microeconomics, which as its name betrays is concerned only with small matters, and that the term 'marginal' in economics is synonymous with unimportant. Nor do I share the current perception, widely held by both professionals and laymen, that trade policies are a specialized fringe issue in Western countries today. Together with public finance, they form the central core of resource allocation questions; and for reasons I have just outlined, I believe that the way in which governments handle these questions is probably the main single influence on the wealth of nations.

Notes

1 Cf. T.W. Hutchison, *The Politics and Philosophy of Economics*, Oxford, Blackwell, 1981, chapter 3.
2 Quoted in Samuel Brittan, *The Role and Limits of Government*, London, Temple Smith, 1983, p. 105. Brittan suggests that these words may have been drafted by Callaghan's son-in-law, Peter Jay, and adds that 'Callaghan himself quickly dropped this line of argument.'
3 Douglas Rimmer, *The Economics of West Africa*, London, Weidenfeld and Nicolson, 1984, p. 266.

6

MARKETS, STATES AND ECONOMICS

The Prime Minister *[Mrs Thatcher]: The Government certainly believe in market forces. I believe that the Hon. Member's question relates to the price of North Sea oil. We have certainly been trying to keep down the price increase in oil – rightly so – and for the month of January we were not prepared to allow the price to go higher than $29.75 . . . (House of Commons proceedings, 7 February 1980)*

In my previous lectures I have contrasted two ways of looking at economic systems and choices. One is the orthodox economic view, which emphasizes the role of prices and markets. Not all economists accept it, and some of those who do are inclined to stress its limitations, or even its dangers. None the less it is distinctively, characteristically professional. The other view of the world is that of do-it-yourself economics. I have shown that the ideas of DIYE remain influential, as they always have been; and I have questioned them both as a description of reality and as a guide to economic policy. I have argued that generally speaking countries, both rich and poor, would be better off in material terms if their governments relied more on prices and markets, including international markets in particular, and less on administrative regulations and controls; and I gave reasons for believing that this is a more important aspect of economic policy than some of my professional colleagues are inclined to think.

In this final chapter, I shall be setting these arguments in a wider context, and considering political as well as economic aspects.

The Conservative government and the market

Let me start by using a particular illustration to make two general points. At various stages in these lectures I have referred to recent or current British economic policies, drawing on a range of illustrations relating to energy, industry and trade. In every case I noted that these are established policies, pursued by successive governments regardless of party, and that they can be seen to have been influenced by the ideas of do-it-yourself economics. They have not changed since 1979. The notion that Mrs Thatcher and those of her ministers who share her views are ardent and consistent devotees of nineteenth century economic liberalism is mistaken. Over wide areas of policy, they are convinced interventionists.

This, of course, is only part of the picture. It is clear that a number of ministers, including the Prime Minister herself, respond favourably to some of the ideas of economic orthodoxy. Moreover, there are several respects in which British economic policy since 1979 has become notably more market oriented – in fact, the government has gone further than I for one expected. In particular, there is the abolition of exchange control; the reform of trade union and labour laws; legislation against professional monopolies; deregulation, as for example in the bus industry; and – ugly but useful term – privatization. Reforms have also been introduced, or are in prospect, in the broad interconnected areas of taxation and social security. All this adds up to a considerable programme, which is still going ahead. In a House of Commons debate in May 1985, a minister actually went so far as to say that protectionism creates problems rather than solving them, and to hint that the

Multi-Fibre Arrangement might not be an appropriate device to keep in place for ever. This indeed was a significant break with established DIYE doctrine, which was ill received on both sides of the House of Commons. In the macroeconomic sphere, the government's refusal to experiment with an incomes policy is a departure from Conservative as well as Labour precedent, and is linked with the belief that such a policy impedes the working of markets.

At the same time, it has to be borne in mind that there are areas besides energy, industry and trade in which there has been little change – for example, agriculture, town planning and land use, and (apart from the sale of council houses) the highly regulated and controlled housing market. Even privatization does not necessarily mean much. As critics have pointed out in relation to the sale of British Telecom, and the proposed sale of the British Gas Corporation, there is not much purpose in privatizing unless more competitive conditions are created. It is not clear that the government has fully appreciated this point – and of course, the easier it is for a newly privatized corporation to make monopoly profits, the higher the selling price which the government can hope to receive for it.

All in all, there has been substantial continuity, as well as some significant changes of direction, in British economic policy under Mrs Thatcher. Even on the macroeconomic side, where the government has been most widely criticized, it is worth recalling that both money supply targets and public expenditure cash limits were brought in by the previous Labour government. As for resource allocation – that second tier of economic issues on which I have focused attention in these lectures – it is the absence of change in policy, rather than the new departures, which is more striking. In part, this can be explained by tactical considerations, relating to public acceptability and to the balance of power within the Cabinet and the Conservative Party.

But the main single reason for continuity is that ministers, so far from being slaves to laissez-faire dogma, are influenced by the characteristic beliefs and perceptions of do-it-yourself economics.

Mr MacQuedy's politics

The two general points which recent British developments illustrate are these. First, DIYE is bipartisan. Its influence extends, as it generally has in past history, right across the conventional political spectrum. Since I have stressed its universal appeal, this is not a very startling conclusion. My second point is that those who are influenced by orthodox economic ideas have no pre-assigned place on the spectrum – left, right or centre. Contrary to what is often supposed, my fictional orthodox colleague Mr MacQuedy, who favours market-oriented economic policies, is not a man of the right. He holds no firm party political allegiance, and in most if not all the OECD countries he would have to be classed as a floating voter.

At first sight this may seem strange. After all, for many decades it has been socialist parties that have constituted the political left in Western countries; and socialists in particular have stressed the injustices and inefficiencies which may arise from unregulated competitive markets, and argued the case for collective action to prevent or remedy this. Again, greater reliance on prices and markets, which Mr MacQuedy broadly supports, goes together with what has been termed 'rolling back the frontiers of the state'; and this is a cause which Mrs. Thatcher and President Reagan, among other political leaders who are classed as conservative or right of centre, have declared as their own. These considerations suggest that orthodox economic ideas go together with political conservatism.

This, however, is not the whole story. Mr MacQuedy is no Marxist, and of course he rejects any presumption that markets are anti-social. In that respect he is definitely not a man of the left. But there are different kinds of socialist in the Western world today, and some of these share his concern with individual welfare and his perception of the ways in which markets can help to promote it. Moreover, generalized hostility to the market economy is by no means confined to the left, as witness – among a long list of possible examples from history – the two Spanish military dictatorships that I mentioned in my last lecture. Mr MacQuedy is against collectivism whatever ideological colours it happens to wear; and as we have seen, he is likewise a sharp critic of economic nationalism, a creed which is embraced at least as warmly on the right as on the left.

As to rolling back the frontiers of the state today, it is not only governments wearing a conservative label that have shown themselves ready to follow this course. In my last lecture I referred to the broad economic strategy which the OECD countries generally have adopted, and which includes maintaining firm control of the money supply, limiting both public expenditure and fiscal deficits, and reducing the extent of official regulations and controls. This strategy has been adopted by left-of-centre governments in Australia, France, Spain, Sweden and – most recently and dramatically – in New Zealand, where it was in fact the election of a Labour government in 1984 which made possible a whole series of moves towards a less controlled economy. In today's world, there is no simple and predictable relationship between party labels and the direction of change in economic policies.

The fact that different Western governments have recently been moving on broadly similar lines does not of course mean that economic policy has ceased to be a matter of controversy – far from it. But it would be wrong to think of the controversy as being between right wing parties which have embraced pro-market orthodox economic ideas and left wing parties which draw their economic inspiration

from other sources, whatever these may be. The controversies are within parties as much as between them.

I want now to explore these issues further, and in doing
so to bring another label more into the picture. Although
Mr MacQuedy is not a party man, something can none the
less be said about his political position – and mine too. The
viewpoint that he and I share is that of economic *liberalism* –
where the term 'liberal' is spelt with a small initial 'l', and
used in its European rather than its American sense, so that
it is not identified with left-of-centre views. We are spiritual
descendants of the great liberal thinkers of the eighteenth
and nineteenth centuries, for whom economic and political
freedom were interrelated goals. Our votes are cast
pragmatically, and not necessarily on the basis of economic
considerations alone, for whatever individuals or parties
seem likely to advance and defend the liberal cause as we
see it.

This cause is not a popular one, precisely because of its
emphasis on the role of prices and markets. The numerous
critics of the market economy are to be found on both the
left and the right, and include economists as well as
laymen. It is in the context of these criticisms that I want to
offer a final variation on my central theme, the contrast
between economic ideas of different kinds and origins.

Laissez-faire, markets and governments

The objections to economic liberalism and the market
economy centre round the role of governments and states,
both nationally and internationally. For many people
liberalism goes with laissez-faire, which in turn is viewed as
outdated, negative, unconcerned with what happens to
weaker members of society and *de facto* favouring the
stronger, and uncompromisingly negative in its attitude to
the state. This rests on a double misconception. First, it
distorts the message of laissez-faire. Second, it wrongly

identifies belief in a market economy with an extreme interpretation of the laissez-faire principle.

As to the first point, laissez-faire gets an undeservedly bad press. The message it conveys is not that governments should be inert or indifferent. Its emphasis is a positive one. It is concerned with economic freedom, including the freedom of individuals and enterprises to enter industries or occupations, to choose their place of residence or operation within a country, and to decide their own products, processes and markets. There is nothing outdated about these principles, nor do they operate against the weak. To the contrary, they enable opportunities to be opened up more widely, and thus operate against special privileges within an economic system. It is no accident that outside the communist world the economy which most conspicuously departs from laissez-faire is that of the Republic of South Africa.

In any case, liberalism is not to be identified with hostility to the state, nor with a doctrinaire presumption that governments have only a minor role in economic life. On the contrary, the liberal view of the role of the state, both internal and external, is strongly positive.

As to internal affairs, governments are seen as having responsibilities which go well beyond the maintenance of order and the provision of collective goods such as national defence. In particular, the active involvement of public authorities is often needed if markets are to function competitively, and in ways that do not produce unwanted side-effects. The right balance between intervention and laissez-faire will vary from case to case, and is always a matter of judgement. Again, governments have to concern themselves with the distribution of income and wealth, though the way in which that concern should be expressed is open to debate. Further, national governments are responsible for the conduct of monetary and fiscal policies, and more generally for trying to ensure conditions in which broad macroeconomic developments will be satisfactory.

There is no automatic guiding formula for this. It requires the continuous exercise of judgement, based on informed professional analysis.

Turning to the international aspect, acceptance of liberal ideas does not at all imply a downgrading of the status or functions of the national state. It is true that those who favour a market economy also favour, as part of their system of belief, a liberal international economic order in which broadly speaking both trade and payments are free from official regulations. But while any move in this direction naturally reduces the sphere of government activity, even the freest of international régimes does not – contrary to what is often alleged – involve an undermining of sovereignty, still less a loss of national identity. Proof of this is to be found in the half century or so preceding the First World War. During this period international transactions of all kinds were largely free from restrictions, but this did not at all mean that the role of national states was eroded. Then as now, the international system was primarily a system of states. The political significance of frontiers was not diminished by the fact that, generally speaking, goods, money and people could move across them unhindered.

In this connection, I myself believe that the national state has an indispensable role in preserving and extending liberal institutions. Where freedom and democracy now exist, they are the creations of particular national sovereign entities, with well-defined geographical boundaries. Their survival depends on the continued existence of such states, and the readiness of the governments and peoples concerned to resist if necessary coercion and violence on the part of other states.

Economic order and disorder

So far from liberals having a doctrinaire bias against the state, it is their more innocent critics, under the sway of intuitive economic ideas, who are prone to accept unquestioningly that centrally devised policies and strategies are both necessary and effective. This goes with a number of interrelated states of mind. One is the unreflecting centralism which I described in my third lecture. A second is a failure to visualize the potential co-ordinating role of prices and markets: it is simply assumed that a coherent set of outcomes can be achieved only through conscious central design. Third, there is the naive but widely accepted belief that actions undertaken from motives of self-interest in general, and profitability in particular, cannot be expected to produce beneficial results. Finally, there is the untested assumption that market mechanisms function in such a way as to increase the extent of inequality, both within countries and between rich and poor states. One aspect of this is the widely shared pre-economic conviction that free trade benefits only the stronger and more advanced nations.

From these mutually supporting notions comes a view of market processes as anarchic, amoral, ineffective and biased against the weak. This view does not involve a conscious rejection of the orthodox economists' vision of reality, but rather a lack of awareness of what this vision comprises.

By contrast, from the liberal point of view it is the market economy, together with the framework of laws and institutions that enables it to function effectively, which serves to establish order, while *ad hoc* discretionary interferences by governments are a source of disorder. In one sense economic liberalism can be said to go against the laissez-faire principle, since it argues that the freedom of governments to act should be constrained by explicit rules and principles. The case for this is political as well as economic.

Of the many examples which could serve to illustrate this point, let me refer again to established bipartisan British official policies in relation to North Sea oil. In general, licences to operate in the British sector of the North Sea are awarded on a discretionary basis. Governments prefer this, largely because it gives them greater control – not just of the award of the licences but over the whole sequence of exploration, development, production and disposal of oil. In particular, they can favour British oil companies and British offshore suppliers, promote specific oil-related developments within Britain, and ensure if need arises that preference is given to British refiners and consumers. To renounce the possibility of exercising such control would be widely regarded as irresponsible.

The effect, however, is to establish a condition of chronic absence of order. This has two main aspects. The first of these is fiscal. The award of discretionary licences means that valuable property rights are handed over without charge. In order to recover as much as possible of the subsequent gains made by the recipients, a special and highly complex tax régime has been set up, which inevitably has become the subject of constant amendments and revisions. Here is a summary description of the main changes in this régime over the period of less than ten years during which it has been in operation:

> Governments were tinkering with the Petroleum Revenue Tax (PRT) almost from the time it began to yield revenue in 1976–77, in efforts to squeeze more out of the oil companies. The rate of PRT has increased from 45% to 60%, then to 70% and again to 75%; and time limits have been placed on both the 'uplift' and 'safeguard' provisions of PRT. Supplementary Petroleum Duty was introduced in the 1981 Budget. It was subsequently replaced by Advance PRT (APRT) which itself is now being phased out. The 'uplift' allowance for capital expenditure has been reduced from 175% to 135%, and payment of PRT has twice been accelerated. For fields defined as 'new', the tax-free oil allowance, which was halved in 1979, was restored to its initial level in the 1983 Budget, while royalty payments were abolished at the same time. No doubt this is far from being the end of the story.[1]

The result of all this is that the profits of the companies are only loosely related to their own performance and to the price of oil, which are the incentives that ought to operate, but instead largely depend on their success in the continuing sequence of tax negotiations.

A second effect of the discretionary system is that the companies are permanently open to pressures from the government, since their chances of getting further licence awards without having to pay for them depend on what is officially seen as good behaviour; and these pressures are often brought to bear in ways that are not fully disclosed, since the government would find it embarrassing to come clean. Even if the pressures were exercised to some worth-while national purpose, which I have argued they are not, this would still be a disturbing state of affairs.

Here as in so many cases in virtually every country, economic policy is viewed, and indeed consciously designed, as an unending series of complicated, opportunist, semi-political deals. Within countries, the effects of this are not only to slow down economic progress but to corrupt political life. On the wider international scene these same conceptions of national interest and of how economic policy is to be viewed lead to continuing and avoidable friction between governments. Liberal trade policies do not in the least guarantee peace, any more than in themselves they ensure rapid economic progress. But they help to restrict areas and grounds of international antagonism, and make for a more ordered as well as a more prosperous world.

The professional critics

So far, in comparing the ideas of economic liberalism with those of its critics, I have been concerned with the objections to the liberal approach which are characteristically made by laymen rather than by economists themselves. But of course there is a widely held professional point of view, to which I referred in my last lecture, that governments have been moving too far towards allowing outcomes to be decided by markets. This in turn is attributed to the influence of economists' ideas, which (it is argued) are based on a mistaken view of how economic systems actually work.

This line of argument is not necessarily incompatible with what I have been saying in these lectures. As to differing views of the system, and of the leading issues of policy – mainly macroeconomic ones – that are involved, I have not taken sides. In any case, it may well be that typically governments rely too much on markets in some areas of policy, and too little in others. However, I find it hard to take seriously those who argue in broad and unqualified terms that present-day governments around the world are in danger of falling too much under the influence of liberal ideas. Although the analogy is not exact, such people put me in mind of those who hold that wearing seat belts in cars is wrong, because it is possible to imagine certain kinds of accidents where this would increase the risk. The bias is the other way. In virtually every country there is a strong built-in tendency to restrict the sphere of markets, because it is the ideas of DIYE that largely rule the world. This is the aspect of reality that I have chosen to emphasize, because my own experience has impressed it on me, and because I believe that it has not been sufficiently recognized.

The limitations of orthodoxy

I want to end this final lecture, as I ended my first one, with some personal reflections on the limitations and uses of economics in general, and orthodox economic ideas in particular, as a guide to the interpretation of events and the choice and design of actual policies.

Let me begin by emphasizing what I have not said, and

do not believe. At no point in these lectures have I argued or implied that the world's economic problems – still less its wider social problems – would be solved if universal free markets prevailed, or if power were safely lodged in the hands either of economists certified as orthodox or of political leaders who relied on such people. It is true that I have made a case for wider recognition of the role of prices and markets, especially in the international sphere, and that this case rests on economic ideas. But I have not presented either the ideas themselves or the changes in direction that they would lead to as a panacea. It is in fact a profound mistake to suppose that complex social and economic issues are like the clues to crossword puzzles, so that specific and lasting solutions to them can be identified.

Just as economics does not offer solutions, so economic analysis in itself cannot provide a detailed blueprint for the actual conduct of affairs. As I stressed in my first lecture, general economic reasoning is only one element in the understanding of a real-life issue or problem; and – let me now add – understanding, even where it can actually be achieved, is no more than a prelude to action. The action itself often has to be decided under the pressure of more or less unexpected events. A distinguished British economist, Sir Alec Cairncross, has recently pointed to the distinction between 'the theorists who seek to trap the inner secrets of the economy in their models and the practitioners who live in a world of action where time is precious, understanding is limited, nothing is certain, and noneconomic considerations are always important and often decisive'.[2] In these lectures I have been largely concerned with general ideas, though I have provided specific illustrations for them. I have said little about the considerable problems that arise in translating such ideas into practice, and which would remain even if economists were more agreed than they are.

Another consideration is that orthodox economic ideas extend to only a part of individual and social life. The orthodox system focuses on individual agents who are seeking economic advantage. It views their thoughts and actions, and their relationships with others, in terms of transactions which are subject to more or less systematic calculation with a view to maximizing probable gains. It draws attention to the ways in which markets can enable these transactions to be conducted more effectively, so that economic goals are more fully realized, and it looks for ways in which the sphere of markets can be extended. I believe, and have argued in these lectures, that this emphasis is justified. At the same time, there is a risk of overdoing it. At the individual level, the picture of human beings as rational maximizers is a caricature, albeit perhaps a useful one. For this and other reasons, I think there is a tendency for orthodox economists to overstate the extent to which societies both are and can be governed by motives of self-interested calculation. In this I part company with my friend Mr MacQuedy, who finds my attitude to these questions somewhat lacking in professional rigour. Rightly or wrongly, I am less of an imperialist for my subject than he is.

By way of final disclaimer, let me take up again the point that I made at the end of my first lecture. Just as I make no extravagant claims for market-orientated policies and the ideas which lend support to them, so the claims that I do make are not dependent on a favourable view of the progress of economics as a discipline. I have called these lectures *Innocence and Design*, where the innocence refers to intuitive economic ideas, and the design to the elaborate system of thought and inquiry which orthodox economics has built up over many decades. But though I think the contrast is valid, I am not arguing that the orthodox design is either grand or complete, nor even that it is evolving in an orderly and systematic way. The very fact that economics is such a divided profession suggests that its status and progress are open to debate.

So I have no starry-eyed view either of what economics has achieved as an academic discipline, nor of what it can offer as a guide to immediate action in the uncertain and rapidly changing situations of real life. Nor have I glossed over the differences of opinions within the subject. It has to be acknowledged that economists are unable to provide agreed answers to a wide range of questions on which people naturally look to them for guidance, and that in economics, even more perhaps than in other disciplines, the advice that political and business leaders receive from the professionals will depend on whom they ask.

Reasons for being a constructivist

All this, however, does not alter the fact that in these lectures I have been concerned to emphasize the uses rather than the limitations of my subject. One of the many possible ways of classifying economists is to distinguish 'constructivists' from sceptics. The constructivists recognize that orthodox economic analysis is not all-embracing, but they choose none the less to emphasize its usefulness in relation to issues of policy, and to underline the dangers of ignoring or going against it. By contrast, the sceptics acknowledge that the orthodox approach is both elegant and helpful within its limits, but they prefer to stress the narrowness of these limits, and the inadequacy of the approach both as a guide to social reality and as a basis for deciding policy. Rather to my surprise my working experience, in a variety of situations and countries, has led me to become an increasingly staunch constructivist, though for the reasons I have just sketched out I am on the sceptical wing of the party. My allegiance has both a negative and a positive side.

The negative aspect has provided the main single theme of these lectures. I have argued that economic analysis can make a major contribution, both to clearer understanding and to the framing of actual policies, in so far as it displaces pre-economic ways of thinking. In particular, the orthodox economic approach offers an alternative to the mutually reinforcing centralist, nationalist and mercantilist assumptions of do-it-yourself economics. I have dwelt on this, since it is in the international sphere preeminently that current official policies, in rich and poor countries alike, are influenced by conceptions of how economic systems work, and where national interests lie, which do not bear informed scrutiny.

As to the positive side, there are two points that I would stress. The first applies to economists in general, rather than constructivists in particular. Two advantages of an economic training are the readiness and ability to think in terms of interdependence and system effects, and a concern with quantitative evidence and ways of interpreting it. In both these respects, as I have indicated at various points in these lectures, DIYE is typically and often unknowingly deficient.

I would make a further claim, broader and more personal, for what I have termed the orthodox economic approach in particular. Economics is not the whole of life, nor is economic policy a purely technical exercise. With economics, as indeed with any subject or system of thought which is concerned with human affairs, it has to be asked not only how far it illuminates its own particular area, but also whether it contributes to a wider understanding. I believe that the orthodox approach throws light on questions that go beyond economics, and that it provides a vantage point for assessing both economic and non-economic aspects of events and choices. Of course, the intellectual traffic is not in one direction only: economics, particularly in its application to policy, will always have much to learn from other disciplines. But the orthodox framework of thought has I think a central strategic position in the realm of ideas. I would claim for it that it enables many of the issues of social and economic life to be seen in clearer perspective, and with a juster sense of proportion. In the complex, uncertain and dangerous world that we inhabit, this claim is not to be despised.

Notes

1 I owe this summary account to Colin Robinson.
2 Sir Alec Cairncross, 'Economics in Theory and Practice', *American Economic Review*, May 1985.

SUGGESTIONS
FOR READING

There is no handy guide to the range of topics referred to in these lectures, while a true bibliography could extend virtually without limit. Here is a short annotated list of books and articles which bear directly on the subject matter of particular lectures, to which I have added a brief personal selection of writings on economic history. I have made half-a-dozen suggestions, some of them covering related works, under each of five headings. I have also listed at the end some of the articles in which I have previously dealt with different aspects of my central theme in these lectures – aspects which range from British nuclear power programmes to the Brandt Report on the reform of the international economic order.

Lecture 1. On the relation between economic ideas and policy:

1   Arthur Seldon (ed.), *The Emerging Consensus* (London, Institute of Economic Affairs, 1981). A book of 'essays on the interplay between ideas, interests and circumstances in the first 25 years of the [Institute]'.

2   Charles Wilson, *Economic History and the Historian: Collected Essays* (London, Weidenfeld and Nicolson, 1969). Chapter 9 is an illuminating essay on 'Government Policy and Private Interest in Modern English

History'. The author, who broadly supports Keynes's famous assertion, makes the point that private inter- ested parties are not *just* pressure groups, but generally have specialized knowledge and evidence which needs to be brought to bear.

3   T.W. Hutchison, *On Revolutions and Progress in Economic Knowledge* (Cambridge, Cambridge University Press, 1978), in which chapter 10 is especially relevant. I also much enjoyed the same author's later volume, *The Politics and Philosophy of Economics* (Oxford, Blackwell, 1981).

4   Sir Alec Cairncross, 'Academics and Policy Makers', chapter 1 of *Changing Perceptions of Economic Policy*, edited by Frances Cairncross (London, Methuen, 1981). Some perceptive comments on this piece are made by John Wright at the end of the chapter.

5   Herbert Stein, *Presidential Economics* (New York, Simon and Shuster, 1984), an admirable account of the evolution of economic policy in the US and the role of economists (and others) in relation to it – especially good on the Nixon period, when the author was himself a member of the Council of Economic Advisers.

6   A.W. Coats (ed.), *The Classical Economists and Economic Policy* (London, Methuen, 1971), an interesting set of essays with a good editorial introduction, centred on the United Kingdom in the first half of the nineteenth century.

Lectures 2–4. Since economists like other professionals are concerned mainly with each other's ideas, studies which throw light on the characteristic differences between their ways of thinking and those of laymen are not too common. From this point of view, I consider two widely different books outstanding:

1   Charles J. Hitch and Roland N. McKean (with others), *The Economics of Defense in the Nuclear Age* (Cambridge, Massachusetts, Harvard University Press, 1960). Chapters 7 and 9–13 provide the best general account I know of the uses of economic analysis in relation to questions of resource allocation, and the reasons why the economist's approach makes better sense than some widely accepted alternatives.

2   P.J.D. Wiles, *Communist International Economics* (Oxford, Blackwell, 1968), a book which goes wider than its title might suggest. (Referred to in chapter 2 above.)

In addition, the following throw light on the difference between these two worlds of economics, lay and orthodox, in different but readable ways.

3   Samuel Brittan, *Is there an Economic Consensus? An Attitude Survey* (London, Macmillan, 1971) makes ingenious use of answers to questions from economics examination papers to show how economists and laymen differ in their approach, and to explore some differences within the profession itself. The same author's essay, *Participation without Politics* (London, Institute of Economic Affairs, 2nd edition 1979) sets out clearly, with well-chosen illustrations, the case for a market economy.

4   There was a lively exchange between Deepak Lal (free trade economist) and Edmund Dell (politician, historian and unashamed mercantilist) in the journal, *The World Economy*, during 1978 and 1979.

5   A recent report from the House of Lords Select Committee on Overseas Trade is interesting and pertinent, as also is much of the evidence submitted to the Committee, two excerpts from which are quoted in chapter 4 above. (House of Lords, Session 1984–85, London, HMSO, 1985.)

6   W.M. Corden, 'Tell Us Where the New Jobs Will Come

from', *The World Economy*, June 1985, deals clearly and briefly with employment and trade issues, from a viewpoint much the same as mine.

The last three items bear particularly on my argument in chapter 4. Items (4) and (5) have the advantage of containing well-formulated statements of the point of view which I have criticized there.

Lecture 5. There is a vast array of works bearing on current macroeconomic controversies. Two contrasted but equally readable sources are:

1 Arjo Klamer, *The New Classical Macroeconomics: Conversations with New Classical Economists and Their Opponents* (Brighton, Wheatsheaf Books, 1984).

2 Samuel Brittan, *The Role and Limits of Government: Essays in Political Economy* (London, Temple Smith, 1983).

On economic development, and the relations between trade policies, the international economic system and economic progress in developing countries, a masterly treatment is:

3 Ian M.D. Little, *Economic Development: Theory, Policy and International Relations* (New York, Basic Books, 1982).

The role of international trade in economic development, and the comparative merits of more open and more insulated economies for developing countries, are considered in an illuminating way in:

4 Irving B. Kravis, 'Trade as a Handmaiden of Growth: Similarities between the Nineteenth and Twentieth Centuries', *Economic Journal*, December 1970.

5 An exchange of views between Professors K.N. Raj and Bela Balassa, to be found in Edmond Malinvaud (ed.),

Economic Growth and Resources: Volume I: *The Major Issues* (London, Macmillan, 1979, pp. 157–76).

The role of pressure groups ('distributional coalitions') as a brake on economic progress forms the main theme of a notable study:

6 Mancur Olson, *The Rise and Decline of Nations* (New Haven, Yale University Press, 1982).

Lecture 6. An excellent short discussion of some fundamental issues touched on in this chapter is:

1 Kenneth J. Arrow, *The Limits of Organization* (New York, W.W. Norton, 1974).

On liberalism today, political and economic, the outstanding work remains:

2 F.A. Hayek, *The Constitution of Liberty* (London, Routledge and Kegan Paul, 1960). A good recent account of Hayek's system of thought as a whole is to be found in John Gray, *Hayek on Liberty* (Oxford, Blackwell, 2nd edition, 1986).

Two successive Hirsch Memorial lectures at the University of Warwick have reviewed in different ways the role and limitations of market mechanisms, and are themselves referred to in a more recent article on the same theme:

3 Frank Hahn, 'Reflections on the Invisible Hand', *Lloyds Bank Review* no. 144, 1982; Amartya Sen, 'The Profit Motive', *Lloyds Bank Review* no. 147, 1983; and Thomas Wilson, 'Invisible Hands: Public and Private', chapter 4 of *Public Sector and Political Economy Today*, edited by Horst Hannuch, Karl W. Roskampf and Jack Wiseman (Stuttgart and New York, Gustav Fischer Verlag, 1985).

The list of works on the status, scope, progress and usefulness of economics is long and hard to choose from. Two stimulating though very different recent contributions are:

4 Lester Thurow, *Dangerous Currents: The State of Economics* (Oxford, Oxford University Press, 1983).

5 Mark Blaug, *The Methodology of Economics, or how economists explain* (Cambridge, Cambridge University Press, 1980).

Finally, as to the role of economists as advisers, and the kinds of knowledge, training and insight which are helpful in performing their role, I would mention in particular two articles:

6 Sir Henry Phelps Brown, 'The Radical Reflections of an Applied Economist', *Banca Nazionale del Lavoro Quarterly Review* no. 132, March 1980; and Sir Alec Cairncross, 'Economics in Theory and Practice', *American Economic Review*, May 1985, quoted in chapter 6 above.

Economic history. Two short, wide-ranging and enlightening books, in each of which markets appear as a leading actor on the historical stage, are:

1 Douglass C. North and Robert Paul Thomas, *The Rise of the Western World* (Cambridge, Cambridge University Press, 1973).

2 Sir John Hicks, *A Theory of Economic History* (Oxford, Clarendon Press, 1969).

An excellent short review of the course of economic history in the OECD countries, especially notable for its ample and lucid statistical documentation, is:

3 Angus Maddison, *Phases of Capitalist Development* (Oxford, Oxford University Press, 1982).

Two illuminating concise surveys of particular historical phases are:

4   Gottfried Haberler, *The World Economy, Money and the Great Depression* (Washington, DC, American Enterprise Institute, 1976).

5   J. F. Wright, *Britain in an Age of Economic Management* (Oxford, Oxford University Press, 1980).

Last, it is worth noting that to do-it-yourself economics there corresponds an equally influential intuitive perception of the course of economic history, in which capitalism, markets and laissez-faire appear as associated villains, or at any rate as sources of unnecessary hardship or waste. Among the studies which cast doubt on this view of events, I especially enjoyed:

6   Barbara Lewis Solow, *The Land Question and the Irish Economy, 1870–1903* (Cambridge, Massachusetts, Harvard University Press, 1971).

On the subject matter of these lectures, I have written about (i) *the role of economists* in the 1961 paper referred to in chapter 1, and also in 'Some Unsettled Issues in Cost-Benefit Analysis', a chapter in Paul Streeten (ed.), *Unfashionable Economics: Essays in Honour of Lord Balogh* (London, Weidenfeld and Nicolson, 1970). I have reviewed (ii) *particular British expenditure programmes* in 'Two British Errors: their Probable Size and Some Possible Lessons', *Oxford Economic Papers*, July 1977; and in 'Nuclear Power in Britain: The Case for a New Approach', *Public Money*, September 1981; and (iii) *British industrial policy* in Charles Carter (ed.), *Industrial Policy and Innovation* (London, Heinemann, 1981) and in 'Problems of Industrial Recovery', *Midland Bank Review*, spring 1982; written in collaboration with Sir Alec Cairncross and Z.A. Silberston. (iv) *Trade policies* are considered in 'Trade Policies and

"Strategies": the Case for a Liberal Approach', *The World Economy*, November 1982; and in 'Trade Policies: Trends, Issues and Influences', *Midland Bank Review*, autumn 1983. I have treated the wider problems of (v) *reforming the international economic order* in 'New Thoughts on a New International Order', *ODI Review*, no. 2 1977; and in 'Survival, Development and the Report of the Brandt Commisssion', *The World Economy*, June 1980. The remarks made in passing in chapter 6 above on (vi) *the role of the state* draw on my contribution, entitled 'National States and the International System', to *Protectionism and Growth* (Geneva, European Free Trade Association, 1985).